The Rise and Fall of Abacus Banking in Japan and China

The Rise and Fall of Abacus Banking in Japan and China

Yuko Arayama and Panos Mourdoukoutas

QUORUM BOOKS
Westport, Connecticut • London

Library of Congress Cataloging-in-Publication Data

Arayama, Yuko, 1951–
    The rise and fall of abacus banking in Japan and China / Yuko Arayama, Panos
    Mourdoukoutas.
        p.   cm.
    Includes bibliographical references and index.
    ISBN 1–56720–324–8 (alk. paper)
    1. Banks and banking—Japan.   2. Banks and banking—China.   I. Title.   II.
    Mourdoukoutas, Panos.
    HG3324.A753   2000
    332.1'095121—dc21   99–046055

British Library Cataloguing in Publication Data is available.

Library of Congress Catalog Card Number: 99–046055
ISBN: 1–56720–324–8

First published in 2000

Quorum Books, 88 Post Road West, Westport, CT 06881
An imprint of Greenwood Publishing Group, Inc.
www.quorumbooks.com

Printed in the United States of America

The paper used in this book complies with the
Permanent Paper Standard issued by the National
Information Standards Organization (Z39.48–1984).

10 9 8 7 6 5 4 3 2 1

To Georgios and Michiko

Nature teaches us to pay little heed to what fortune brings, and when we are prosperous to understand that we are unfortunate, and when we are unfortunate not to regard prosperity highly, and to receive unmoved the good things which come from fortune and to range ourselves boldly against the seeming evils which it brings; for all that many regard as good or evil is fleeting, and wisdom has nothing in common with fortune.

—Epicurus

Contents

Exhibits   xi

Preface   xv

Acknowledgments   xix

1. Beyond Non-performing Assets: Abacus Banking   1

**I. The Rise and Fall of Abacus Banking and the Banking
Crisis in Japan**   **17**

2. The Rise of Abacus Banking in Japan   19

3. The Fall of Abacus Banking in Japan   53

4. The Banking Crisis   73

**II. The Rise and Fall of Abacus Banking and the Looming
Banking Crisis in China**   **99**

5. The Rise of Abacus Banking in China   101

6. The Fall of Abacus Banking in China   127

7. The Looming Banking Crisis in China   145

8. Conclusions   163

    Selected Bibliography   171
    Index   179

Exhibits

1.1	Non-performing Loans for Selected Japanese Banks in 1998	3
1.2	Assets Managed per Bank Worker in Japan, China, and the United States (1981–1998)	9
2.1	Economic Plans: Fiscal Years, GNP Growth Target, and Average Annual GNP Growth Achieved (1956–1992)	23
2.2	Real GNP Annual Growth in Major Industrial Countries (1960–1987)	24
2.3	Asset Accumulation and Financial Intermediation in Japan and the United States (1954–1988)	26
2.4	Indirect Financing Ratio (1954–1988)	27
2.5	Bank Deposits in Japan (1960–1996)	28
2.6	Bank Loans in Japan (1960–1996)	30
2.7	Bank Loans in the United States (1980–1995)	31
2.8	International Comparison of Bank Profitability	38
2.9	*Gosou-sendan Houshiki*	43
2.10	Bank Assets, Economic Growth, and *Gosou-sendan Houshiki*	44
3.1	Exchange Rate (1981–1996)	58
3.2	Financing Ratio of Non-financing Firms (percent, 1975–1989)	60
3.3	Interest Rate Spread (1980–1996)	61
3.4	Employment and GDP by Sector in 1995	64

3.5   Japan's Broad Money Supply Growth   66

3.6   Average Tariff Cuts Achieved in the Uruguay Round for
        Industrial Goods   67

3.7   Real GDP Annual Growth in Major Industrial Countries for
        Selected Periods   68

3.8   The Disbanding of *Gosou-sendan Houshiki*   70

4.1   The World's Ten Largest Banks (1982–1998)   75

4.2   Standard & Poor's Long-Term Issue Credit Ratings (1991–1998)   76

4.3   Standard & Poor's Bond Ratings (1986–1997)   77

4.4   Loans Outstanding by Industry (1975–1995)   81

4.5   Bank Deposits, Loans, and GDP (1960–1994)   83

4.6   Production Capacity and Operating Rate (1981–1996)   86

4.7   Purchase versus Sale Value of Selected Japanese Investments   88

4.8   Banks' Latent Profits   89

4.9   Bank Net Loans in Japan (1960–1996)   91

4.10   Bank Net Loans in the United States (1980–1995)   92

4.11   Unemployment Rate (1975–1996)   94

4.12   Japan's Domestic Wholesale Price Index (1981–1996)   95

4.13   Japan's Labor Productivity (1960–1996)   96

5.1   Foreign Direct Investment in China (1983–1997)   109

5.2   Foreign Trade in China (1950–1995)   110

5.3   Real GDP Growth in China (1952–1996)   111

5.4   Financial Organization in China   112

5.5   China's Savings (1991–1995)   114

5.6   Bank Loans in China (1980–1997)   115

5.7   Bank Loans in the United States (1980–1995)   116

5.8   Bank Assets (1980–1997)   118

5.9   Financial Assets Distribution (1986–1994)   120

5.10   Bank Deposits in China (1980–1997)   121

5.11   Bank Deposits in the United States (1980–1995)   122

6.1   U.S. Trade Deficit with China (1985–1997)   130

6.2   U.S. Demands on China   131

6.3   China's Export Unit Value (1985–1996)   134

6.4   Foreign Direct Investment in China (1995–1997)   136

6.5   China's Trade (1992–1997)   137

6.6	Real GDP Growth (1994–1999)	138
6.7	SOE Profits (1994–1998)	139
6.8	Credit Funds Balance Sheet of State Bank User Funds in 1997	140
6.9	Money Supply of China (1977–1995)	141
7.1	Selected Bank Downgrades as of October 15, 1998	147
7.2	Moody's Credit Rating for Selected ITICs	148
7.3	Debt-to-Equity Ratios of the Mainland Parents of Some Prominent Hong Kong "Red Chips" as of December 31, 1997	149
7.4	Corporations that Missed Bond Payments in 1999	150
7.5	Government Revenues, Expenditures, and Debt Incurred (1970–1995)	152
7.6	Bank Net Loans in China (1980–1997)	154
7.7	Bank Net Loans in the United States (1980–1995)	155
7.8	Production, Employment, and Establishments in the Construction Sector in China (1981–1996)	157
7.9	Annual Growth Rate of Loans in State-Owned Banks by Region (1990–1994)	160

Preface

Complacency is dangerous, especially in a rapidly changing world. For decades, Japanese bankers were complacent with a rapidly growing economy and with cozy relationships with government bureaucrats who pursued policies that virtually eliminated traditional banking risks. Rapid economic growth, for instance, provided a steady flow of deposits, which in turn financed corporate expansion. Rapid economic growth further fueled corporate profits and asset inflation that made the repayment of loans almost a certain bet. But what did make the repayment of loans a certain bet was Japan's industrial policy and tight regulation as practiced by the Ministry of International Trade and Industry (MITI) and the Ministry of Finance (MOF), especially policies bailing out declining industries and limiting competition among banks.

In addition, Japan's government regulators directly controlled the Postal Savings, a government agency, and monitored closely the day-to-day operations of private banks, in essence controlling the behavior of bank managers. In this sense, Japanese banking replicated more the banking of the former socialist countries, where managers were appointed by government bureaucrats and rationed credit according to the priorities of central planning, and less the banking of market economies, where credit is allocated according to the principles of risk management.

Complacency is not confined to Japanese bankers alone. It extends to Chinese bankers, too, if one can talk about Chinese bankers in the market meaning of the term. Under communist rule, Chinese "bankers" have been complacent with government ownership and interest rate controls that turned banking into a government department, an instrument of central planning. Since 1978, Chinese bankers have also been complacent with economic growth, asset appreciation, and government protection that "eliminates" traditional banking risks. Their function is limited to that of government accountants that ration credit according to central planning priorities rather than according to the principles of risk management.

Unconcerned with risk and under tight bureaucratic supervision and control, Japanese and Chinese bankers grew up as abacus bankers, as record keepers of money flows, deriving income from seigniorage, from the passive creation of money through interest-bearing loans rather than from true banking, and from active asset management.[1] In this capacity, banks behave more as welfare agencies that keep afloat inefficient and ineffective corporations, providing employment and income for their employees and supporting community needs, and less as banks in the true meaning of the term. Japanese managers by nature and Chinese managers by social rule are also driven by a herd mentality, moving collectively from one direction to another, causing wild asset price fluctuations that manifest themselves into financial crises. This was particularly true in the late 1980s for Japan and in the early 1990s for China. Japanese and Chinese bankers invested in overvalued real estate, equities, art, and other objects of speculation—assets that they shouldn't have invested in under the basic principles of risk management.

Unfortunately for both Japan and China, rapid economic growth did not last forever; neither did the cozy relations with government bureaucrats. By the late 1980s in Japan and by the mid-1990s in China, economic growth slowed down, global competition intensified, asset values collapsed, and government regulation was partially lifted, especially in Japan. As a result, both Chinese and Japanese bankers found themselves with piles of non-performing assets, scores of competitors invading their home turf, and a tough task to reckon with—learning to behave as true bankers (i.e., how to manage traditional and non-traditional risks).

Arguing this hypothesis, this book claims that, though necessary, an American-style rescue package that cleans the balance sheets of Japanese and Chinese banks is not sufficient to solve the banking woes of the two countries. To be sufficient, any rescue package must set the parameters for true banking (i.e., bank managers must be afforded the opportunity, freedom, and incentives to run banks as for-profit businesses rather than as welfare agencies). Bank managers must further escape the abacus mentality and learn how to use their brains rather than their fingers. They must shift from abacus banking to credit risk management, and that may take much longer than anxious Western observers would have expected.

NOTE

1. Originally, seigniorage (or seignorage) was the sovereign right of a lord or a government to issue money, which in essence was a form of implicit taxation, and therefore a source of income. The size of such income depended upon the difference between the intrinsic and the monetary value of the monetary instruments. Later on, seigniorage was also transferred to banking institutions that could create money through the conventional principle of money multiplier.

Acknowledgments

Part of this book was completed during Panos Mourdoukoutas' stay at Nagoya University and Chukyo University. The authors are indebted to professors Akira Yakita of Chukyo University, Tadashi Yagi of Doshisha University, and Shogo Kimura of Nagoya University, and to Mr. Atsushi Nishiyama and Mr. Katsuya Miyoshi.

The Rise and Fall
of Abacus Banking
in Japan and China

Chapter 1

Beyond Non-performing Assets: Abacus Banking

In the years 1986 to 1991, Japan generated a wave of hyperliquidity. This extraordinary surge of money created one of the great collective madnesses of world financial experience, a speculative excess that created what came to be known as the bubble economy, an event that *Forbes* magazine in 1987 identified as comparable with the notorious Dutch tulip bulb craze of the 17th century or the South Sea bubble of the 18th.

—Peter Hartcher[1]

For decades, Japan's robust economy was the envy of the world. Her export-led industrialization growth strategy served as a role model for growth and prosperity for the emerging economies of nearby Southeast Asia and elsewhere around the world. Her labor institutions and management practices became case studies in MBA programs around the world. Her bureaucrats at the legendary Ministry of International Trade and Industry (MITI) and the Ministry of Finance (MOF) dreamed of taking on the world's largest economy, the United States, especially in the second half of the roaring 1980s, in the "bubble years" when the U.S. and European economies remained stagnant. In fact, according to some Japanese politicians, the country's modern economic model, especially management organization, was an alternative to the antiquated U.S. economic model:

The Japanese way of doing things seems to fit this stage of history better. . . . The Japanese system puts emphasis on stability and teamwork and has distinct advantages. It fits the requirements of the times, particularly of this stage of technological development.[2]

As we enter the new millennium, Japan's sluggish economy is no longer the envy of the world. Her export-led industrialization strategy no longer serves as a role model for the emerging economies in Asia or elsewhere, but as a bad lesson, an example of crony capitalism doomed to economic bubbles and bursts. Her labor institutions and management are losing their popularity with MBA programs around the world. Her bureaucrats at MITI and MOF face the anger and the dismay of their U.S. counterparts for failing to address the economic problems of the country, a failure that has turned into a threat for the global economy. Indeed, Japan's economic performance since the early 1990s, a period of world recovery and robust growth for the U.S. economy, has been disappointing. Real GDP growth fell from 6.1 percent in 1988 to 3.8 percent in 1991, falling into negative territory by 1994. After a 3.5 percent rebound in 1996, it slid into negative territory again in 1998 and expected to grow by 0.6 percent in 1999. In the meantime, the Nikkei stock average dropped from 40,000 in 1989 to below 13,000 by 1998 before returning to 17,000 by mid-1999, while real estate prices returned to their pre-1985 levels.

At the core of Japan's economic woes is a prolonged banking crisis, as manifested in the billions of dollars of non-performing loans which have yet to be written off. Even as recently as 1998, in spite of several government packages, Tokyo Mitsubishi Bank, DKB, Sumitomo Bank, and Sakura have disposed of less than half of their non-performing assets (see Exhibit 1.1).

Japan's banking crisis is also manifested in a credit crunch that has neutralized monetary policy (i.e., aggressive monetary easing has failed to expand lending to allying business sectors of the economy and resolve the banking crisis). As an *Economist* report puts it, "The sickness of Japan's banks makes any macroeconomic approach to the problem, fiscal or monetary, irrelevant; the country's productive potential, not merely its ability to mobilize demand, is collapsing."[3] Indeed, since 1990, the Bank of Japan (BOJ) has launched an unprecedented expansionary monetary policy, lowering the discount rate from 5.5 percent to 0.25 percent without avail. At the same time, the Japanese government has launched an aggressive fiscal stimulus package that poured billions of yen into

Exhibit 1.1
Non-performing Loans for Selected Japanese Banks in 1998

JPY billions

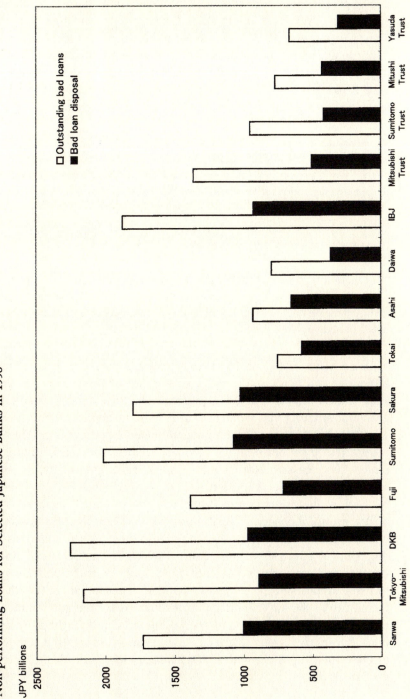

public projects without avail,[4] and the 1996 launching of a Japanese version of the U.S. Resolution Trust Corporation—the Japan Resolution Trust Corporation (JRTC)—has failed to produce any meaningful results.

Burdened with billions of dollars of non-performing assets and striving to meet the Bank International Settlement (BIS) requirements, Japanese banks have opted to invest in domestic and foreign fixed income securities rather than to extend new loans.[5] As Sato puts it:

Weakened to the point of collapse in some cases, Japanese banks have been unable to provide sufficient capital, in the form of loans, to Japanese companies, as they work instead to meet the necessary BIS capital ratios by cutting back on their assets and refusing to renew loans.[6]

The bank's reluctance to extend new loans now dried up financing, especially for start-up enterprises. As McAlinn states:

The magnitude of the bad debt problem facing Japan's banks has led to paralysis where the entire focus is on survival with little attention being paid to the ongoing financing needs of existing business, or to the more critical and higher risk needs of start-up enterprises.[7]

Like a black hole, the Japanese banking system has been absorbing billions of yen in taxpayer money with no improvement in sight. In fact, since the creation of the JRTC, the banking crisis has deepened and the economic situation has worsened. In 1998 in particular, Japan's economic growth turned from sluggish to negative, pushing the country into a true recession and diminishing the recovery chances for Asia's allying economies. The recession also claimed a major political casualty, the erosion of the Liberal Democratic Party's (LDP) power in the Fall 1998 elections that led to the resignation of Prime Minister Ryutaro Hashimoto.

One group of observers attributes Japan's failure to apply successfully an American-style rescue package for resolving its banking crisis to (1) the political paralysis of the country, which has undermined financial markets and consumer confidence; (2) the failure of the political system to place under control the "heavy-handed" bureaucrats at the MOF; (3) the failure to pursue economic policies that are for the good of the country rather than for the good of special interests; and (4) the slow sales of non-performing assets.[8] Hartcher, for instance, blames the interference of *Okurasho* (the MOF) with market forces, especially its efforts to support stock prices:

The *Okurasho* decided that Tokyo stock prices could be allowed to fall no further. In a breathtaking demonstration of its determination, it stepped directly into the marketplace and pitted its power and resources against the world's investors in the second-biggest stock market on earth in the full cry of collapse.[9]

A March 21, 1998 *Economist* editorial attributes the crisis to the Japanese government's failure to restore confidence to Japanese consumers and investors. "Confidence is the key: to persuade consumers to start spending again, to persuade investors, domestic and foreign, that Japan is again (or at last) a country of opportunity."[10] Sharing this view, U.S. Treasury Secretary Robert Rubin observes that the most important key with respect to economic conditions in Japan is to restructure its banking system in an efficient fashion that wins the approval of the world financial markets.

Another *Economist* editorial attributes Japan's failure to implement successfully the American rescue package to the slow sale of nonperforming assets of Japanese banks.[11] Ohmae argues that "the origins of Japan's economic problems were not unique. The government's disastrous response to them was."[12] In particular, Ohmae refers to the overemphasis of the LDP government on fiscal stimulus earmarked for projects in remote areas of the country rather than in urban areas, especially Tokyo, where such spending is needed the most. Ohmae also refers to the failure of the Japanese government to deregulate its economy. Ohmae's view is shared by Friedman, who argues that Japanese policy makers should have focused on a permanent marginal tax rate cut rather than on expansionary government spending.[13]

A second group of observers attributes the problem to the deterioration of the Asian economies and its fallout for the Japanese economy, and the Japanese banks in particular.[14] Watanabe, for instance, argues that Japan's banking crisis is a manifestation of Asia's banking crisis.[15] Fly observes that Asian affiliates of financial institutions share the problems of these countries.[16] Reinebach argues that "the Asian economic crisis has devastated Japanese banks, weakening their already slim capital levels and heightening concern in the minds of investors."[17] The failure of the Guangdong International Trust Corporation (GITC), for instance, left Japanese banks with over $1 billion in bad loan write-offs. Indeed, in early 1999, Sumitomo Bank, Sakura Bank, and Fuji Bank wrote off an estimated $1.29 billion in bad loans.[18]

A third group of economic observers attributes Japan's prolonged crisis to insufficient deficit spending. Krugman, for instance, argues that

Japan's government deficit is structural rather than cyclical. In this sense, the country's banking crisis is the result of economic stagnation rather than the result of deliberate action of the government to stimulate the economy.[19]

A fourth group of observers attributes Japan's prolonged crisis to the "lack of a sense of crisis," which in turn can be attributed to four taboos of the country's financial system: (1) taxpayers are prepared to bail out banks; (2) foreigners should not be kept out of the industry; (3) certain banks are too big to fail; and (4) banks should preserve lifetime employment for their regular employees at any cost.[20]

In this book we argue a fifth contention: An American-style rescue package under way is not a sufficient cure for Japan's banking crisis because Japan's banking system is radically different than that of the United States or Europe. Nurtured under a fast-growing economic environment, "main bank" *keiretsu* relations, and tight government regulation that virtually controlled bank management behavior, eliminated competition, and rationed credit, according to MITI and MOF priorities, Japanese banks have grown up as abacus bankers. Since its inception, especially in the boom years, the Japanese banking system as a whole has been functioning as a record keeper of money flows rather than as a true banker, managing investment risk. The primary difference between now and then appears to be the use of ATM machines replacing abacus-calculators in monitoring the money flows into and out of the banking system.

The same arguments can be made even more forcefully for the looming banking crisis in China. Owned by the "people" and controlled by government and Communist Party bureaucrats, Chinese banks have been run as state-owned enterprises, often collecting government-imposed deposits and rationing funds to various sectors of the economy according to political priorities. In addition, bank lending fills the vacuum created by the erosion of the country's tax base and the shortfall in government revenues and spending associated with it.

Chinese and Japanese "bankers" lack the ability, the capability, and the incentives to run banks as for-profit business. In this sense, Japanese and Chinese bankers completely fail to save not only themselves but also their customers, a serious crime in the Western world. Therefore, cleaning balance sheets from non-performing assets is the necessary but not the sufficient condition for curing the woes of Japanese and Chinese banks. The sufficient condition is threefold:

- Japanese and Chinese managers must behave as for-profit institutions where managers are accountable to the owners and stockholders.

- Japanese and Chinese managers must be freed from government directives (China) and guidance (Japan) that control their day-to-day operations and must restrict their freedom to develop new products and businesses.

- Japanese and Chinese bank managers must learn to behave as true bankers (i.e., learn how to manage financial risks and function as public trading corporations, especially how to deal with transparency and full disclosure rules and regulations, as is the case with their Western counterparts).

Modernizing the corporate governance of the banking institutions of the two countries, freeing bank managers from the control of regulators, and educating them about the principles and the mentality of risk management, in turn, may take many years—perhaps an entire generation rather than a few years, as was the case in the United States.

Abacus banking in Japan can be traced back to the last quarter of the nineteenth century, as a cause and a result of the country's urgent desire to industrialize and catch up with America and Europe. Indeed, under a government policy known as the Policy of Enriched Industrialization and under the 1893 Banking Act, banks were established for the purpose of financing a number of industries chosen for rapid growth. In this sense, banks played a major role in the country's rapid industrialization. Conversely, the country's rapid industrialization played a major role in the development of the banking industry. As a report by the BOJ Research Department puts it:

This modern banking system stimulated the growth of modern industries, which in turn enabled the banking system to develop further and to expand. By the first decade of the twentieth century, when modern industries had taken fairly firm root in Japan, the special banks had been established and the shape of the banking system was more or less complete.[21]

In this sense, "Japanese banks have long discovered that the best way of helping themselves has been to aid industrial growth through medium- and long-term lending as well as by short-term operational loans."[22] Indeed, banks discovered that economic growth helps them in a number of ways. First, it raises income and savings, and therefore it creates a steady flow of deposit funds, especially in the absence of well-organized financial markets. Second, it stimulates corporate investment and the demand for corporate loans, especially in a country where corporations rely heavily on indirect rather than direct financing. Third, economic growth raises corporate revenues and asset values, often placed as collateral for bank loans. Fourth, steady economic growth allows banks to conceal losses in bad years (i.e., losses in bad years would be balanced out by gains in good years).

In addition, as long as the economy grows, bank sector assets as a whole could rise just through seigniorage income (i.e., the passive creation of money through interest-bearing loans rather than the active management of investment risk). Simply put, as long as the economy grows, the best strategy for Japanese banks is to keep on lending money to the industries promoted by the MITI and under the "order" created by the MOF rather than to assign loans according to the principles of risk management. To put it differently, Japanese banks focused on loan volume rather than on loan quality as a competitive strategy. Reflecting this strategy, bank assets per worker increased steadily over the period 1981–1991, compared to the United States, where assets per worker remained roughly constant (see Exhibit 1.2).[23]

Though a high-volume competitive strategy may make sense in any high-growth economy, it makes particularly good sense in economies that meet five additional conditions:

- A steady, positive interest-rate spread.[24]
- Close ties between banks and their corporate clients (relational banking).
- Tight government regulation that controls interest rates, restricts entry to the banking industry, limits competition among banks, controls day-to-day banking operations, and justifies "passive" action.
- A government policy that is prepared to bail out industries and corporations, the major clients of banks.
- Loans are to be extended to tangible assets with a long life, such as conventional manufacturing rather than intangible assets, services or rapidly turning obsolete manufacturing assets, and vice versa. Simply put, abacus banking works better in a manufacturing rather than a service-oriented economy.

A close examination of Japan's economy reveals that, with the exception of the 1920s and the 1930s, the country satisfied all of the above conditions, especially in the extended high growth era that began in the late 1950s and lasted until the bubble economy in the late 1980s. Specifically, over the said period:

Exhibit 1.2
Assets Managed per Bank Worker in Japan, China, and the United States (1981–1998)

Index (1986=100)

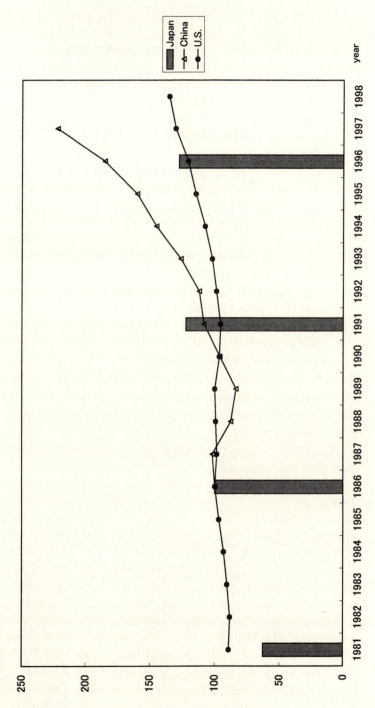

- Corporate governance provided bank managers a "free hand" in managing assets on behalf of the true bank owners. This was especially the case in government-owned financial institutions, such as the Postal Savings, where office heads are appointed in the same way as government officials. Corporate governance further allowed banks to *bogai*, (to "detour") or keep their losses off the formal records.

- To accommodate fast economic growth, the BOJ provided almost unlimited liquidity to banks, eliminating liquidity risk, a traditional banking risk.

- The government intervened in recessions to support hard-hit clients such as the coal, steel, and shipbuilding industries in the mid-1970s. In this way, the government eliminated credit risk, another traditional banking risk.

- The banking industry was under tight regulation, which not only kept newcomers out of the industry but virtually eliminated competition among banks and controlled the behavior of bank managers. In such an environment, government directives took precedence over risk management in allocating banking credit to prospective borrowers.

- Due to savings-biased policies, favorable demographics, and government regulation, Japan's savings rates stayed among the highest in the industrial world, creating a *tsunami*, a high tide of bank deposits that financed the expansion of the corporate sector.

- Assets, mainly land assets normally placed as collateral for bank loans, skyrocketed in value, especially during the bubble economy years.

- Japan's growth was concentrated in manufacturing, especially prior to 1974, where assets were visible and easier to appraise compared to service industries.

Besides, banks' long-term relations with industry groups, known as *keiretsu*, and implicit commitment to enterprise unions to warrant lifetime employment to their regular employees, make it more convenient, even mandatory, for banks to focus on a strategy of money creation, low-interest volume lending. Low-interest *volume* lending allows *keiretsu* members to aggressively expand their sales and market shares and provide stable employment and high wages for their regular employees.[25]

It is no surprise, therefore, that in the high-growth era Japanese banks not only prospered, but reached the summit of the world economy. In the late 1980s, for instance, almost 50 percent of the world's top 20 banks and 60 percent of the world's top ten banks were Japanese.[26] They reached this position without any special effort, any active management of their assets, or any concern about investment risks, but with passive management, abacus banking, and the steady monitoring of fund flows from household depositors to industry borrowers. As Sapsford puts it:

Banks didn't need to worry about whether lending rates accurately reflected risk. They extended all loans—whether to big steel companies or local green grocers—at extremely favorable rates, often just a few percentage points over funding costs. Banks never had to be concerned with raising profits from their loans, they merely competed in terms of *loan volume*. (emphasis added).[27]

Preoccupied with volume rather than risk management, Japanese bankers and their clients were taken by a wild herd mentality, which can find its parallels to the South Sea and Dutch tulip manias. This was particularly the case in the late 1980s, when financial deregulation and the hyperliquidity created by the easy monetary policy after the Plaza Accord challenged abacus banking. Japanese banks, both directly and through their non-bank subsidiaries (*jusen*), rushed to finance the high-profile investment spree that reached for the world trophies, from movie studios to real estate, at any price. But banks were not alone.

Joining banks, the country's corporations sometimes abandoned their traditional productive activities and engaged in *zeitek* (financial alchemy). Japanese collectors paid a record $40 million for Vincent van Gogh's "Sunflowers," Mitsui Real Estate overpaid $235 billion for the Exxon building,[28] and Mitsubishi Real Estate paid $850 million for New York's Rockefeller Center. Worse, ignoring a well-known credit risk management principle of diversification, Japanese banks and other credit institutions limited their lending to a few individuals and institutions. Tokyo-Kyowa, for instance, lent $376 million (or 40 percent of the institution's total outstanding loans) to a Mr. Takahashi, an entrepreneur who had cozy ties with MOF officials. Credit co-ops did even worse than that; close to 40 percent of them extended large loans to single clients, illegally![29]

Unfortunately for Japanese banks, most of the conditions for profitable abacus banking faded away by the late 1980s and the early 1990s. Under a number of foreign and domestic pressures for opening the country's economy to competition, economic growth came down to earth, government regulations that had limited entry and competition in the banking industry began to be lifted, asset prices and savings rates declined sharply, and the economy continued to shift from manufacturing to services. Unexpectedly, Japanese banks found themselves in possession of non-performing assets valued at a fraction of their lending value, far away from the helm of the world economy with billions of yen of non-performing assets, in a new world where true bankers screen loan applicants and assess default risks rather than monitor cash flows with abacus or ATM machines. By 1998, Japanese banks not only rolled down from the summit of the world economy but almost vanished from the world financial markets, "unable to make profit on investment-grade loans."[30] Well-known names, such as Sumitomo Bank, reached to the U.S. financial markets, markets that they had once invaded, for raising $1.8 billion in perpetual preferred stock,[31] and they had to pay a "shameful" "Japan premium" of 1 percent over the standard international borrowing rates. According to a *Euromoney* editorial, "the country is now at danger of losing contact with its supposed peers in the development world."[32]

Though China's growth experience and economic structure have been radically different for the most part of her history than that of Japan, the country's nineteenth-century government- and guilds-regulated banking industry displays two characteristics of abacus banking: tight government regulation, and relational banking. The same is true for the state of the industry during the early communist period, when banks were socialized and turned into government departments within a centrally planned system. In this sense, "banks" played the role of government accountants monitoring the money flows between the government treasury and the corporate sector. But China's banking system turned into a "pure" abacus banking system during the post-1978 market liberalization era, when robust economic growth allowed banks to expand volume lending as reflected in the asset/worker ratio (see Exhibit 1.1). Specifically in the post-1978 era:

- The country experienced rapid and robust economic growth, which boosted savings and bank deposits, often under the government mandate; it further allowed state-owned enterprises (SOEs) and banks to hide their losses.

- Economic growth was concentrated in manufacturing.

- The country experienced rising asset prices.

- By and large, banking remained either under ownership or direct government control, which controlled interest rates, restricted industry entry, and virtually eliminated competition among banks.

- Government bureaucrats and Communist Party leaders generally appointed bank managers who often lacked the freedom and the expertise to manage bank assets in a way other than that dictated by their bosses.

- The government was prepared to bail out ailing SOEs.

- Competition from foreign banks was limited to foreign currency transactions only.

Controlled by government bureaucrats and Communist Party leaders rather than by bank professionals, Chinese banks were preoccupied with maintaining the status quo (i.e., preserving the vested interests of national, provincial, and local Communist and Labor Party leaders) rather than with risk management. Banks extended loans to money-losing SOEs and TVEs (township and village enterprises)—often to pay for wages and benefits to labor in order to preserve the "iron bowl" tradition of the Maoist era—and financed infrastructure projects for the benefit of the local party leaders and their patrons.

Unfortunately, as was the case in Japan, the abacus banking conditions in China did not last forever. By the mid-1990s, especially after the Asian crisis, China's growth began to descend from double to single digits; her markets began to open slowly to competition, and her asset values began to fall. At the same time, in their bid to join the World Trade Organization (WTO), Chinese regulators found themselves under enormous international pressures to privatize SOEs and to deregulate their banking industry, allowing foreign banks to expand their presence outside foreign currency transactions to the domestic sector.

Yet bank managers continued to lack the freedom, the incentive, and the expertise to manage banks as their market counterparts. Worse, in an effort to preserve the status quo at any cost, Chinese banks financed a growth paranoia that called for an acceleration of construction spending, especially in the Southeast regions, which could no longer count on robust exports and foreign investment for growth. Accommodating this construction mania was the setup of credit co-ops and International Trust and Investment Corporations (ITICs), which amassed enormous funds domestically (in the case of credit co-ops) and internationally (in the case of ITICs).

As the economy slowed down, Chinese bank managers, following the footsteps of Japan, began to discover that access to world markets is not just a source of opportunity but a source of risk and uncertainty too. Nevertheless, this did not stop them from expanding credit to their corporate clients, notably to the ailing SOEs. Neither did it stop them from financing commercial and residential real estate construction, though they knew the structures would end up vacant. And although they did not openly admit it in the public, banks also found themselves with billions of dollars of non-performing assets in a risky and uncertain world.

In short, Japan's banking crisis and China's looming banking crisis are more than just a matter of non-performing assets or a matter of political will and determination to deal with ailing banks. It is a matter of the failure of a long-time strategy that reduced banking simply to a record-keeping operation (abacus banking) to adjust to the new environment brought about by globalization and deregulation, especially in the case of China, which comes off a communist system of entitlements and government guarantees. In this sense, unless some of the conditions for abacus banking are reinstated, a rescue package that clears balance sheets from non-performing loans may avert a catastrophe, but it will not solve the problem. Namely, it will not provide for the freedom and the skills to manage risks; it will not teach Japanese and Chinese bankers to behave like true bankers.

What will provide Japanese and Chinese bankers with both the freedom and the skills to manage risks and teach them to behave like true bankers is the transformation of the Japanese and Chinese banks into true for-profit institutions, which, in turn, requires three institutional changes:

- A change in the corporate governance laws in the two countries that will make managers accountable and responsible to their stockholders.
- A change in government regulation that provides managers with the freedom and the incentives to adjust the quantity and the quality of their services in response to changes in market conditions and to introduce new services.
- A change in disclosure, transparency, and accounting practices to allow depositors and stockholders to monitor the performance of banking institutions and to assess the risks and rewards of their investments.

Arguing these contentions in more detail, the remainder of this book contains two parts. Part I discusses the rise and fall of abacus banking in Japan in the postwar period and the banking crisis of the 1990s, and Part II addresses the rise and fall of abacus banking in China and the looming banking crisis of the 1990s.

A chapter-by-chapter discussion follows. Chapter 2 contains a more detailed discussion of the "extended high-growth" era from the early 1950s to the late 1980s and investigates how this era provided the conditions for abacus banking. Chapter 3 presents a discussion of the low-growth, post-bubble era and investigates the decline and fall of abacus banking. Chapter 4 discusses of how the rise and fall of abacus banking contributed to the prolonged banking crisis of the 1990s. Chapter 5 presents the rise of abacus banking throughout China's economic history, especially under communist rule and the post-liberalization, high-growth era (1978–1993). Chapter 6 discusses the decline and fall of abacus banking in the slow-growth era (1995–present). Chapter 7 offers a discussion about how the rise and fall of abacus banking have contributed to the looming banking crisis, and the Chapter 8 summarizes and concludes the preceding discussions.

NOTES

1. Hartcher (1998), p. 62.
2. K. Watanabe, Deputy Foreign Ministry of Economic Affairs, quoted in the *New York Times*, November 10, 1991. Also, see Smith (1994).
3. *The Economist* (1998), p. 17.
4. In April 1998, for instance, the Japanese government launched a 16.65 billion-yen fiscal stimulus package.
5. Japan's purchase of foreign bonds increased from $37.4 billion in 1992 to $91.4 billion by 1995. For details, see OECD (1995), p. 36.
6. Sato (1998), p. 372.
7. McAlinn (1999), p. 6.
8. One reason for the slow sales of non-performing assets is the foreclosure procedures that require the voluntary consent of the property owner. For details, see OECD (1997), p. 46.
9. Hartcher (1998), p. 104.
10. *The Economist*, March 21, 1998, p. 15.
11. "Japanese Banks" (1998).
12. K. Ohmae, "Not Another Hashimoto, Please!" *Newsweek*, July 27, 1998, p. 19.
13. M. Friedman, "Monetary Policy Dominates," *Wall Street Journal*, January 8, 1999.
14. According to some estimates, Japanese banks hold about one-third of the foreign loans of Indonesia, Thailand, and South Korea.
15. Watanabe (1998).
16. R. Fly, "Is Creditor Better than Debtor?" *Wall Street Journal*, January 11, 1999.
17. Reinebach (1998), p. 14.
18. F. Furukawa, "China: Japanese Banks Tighten Further," *Nikkei Weekly*, February 1, 1999, p. 1.
19. P. Krugman, "The Return of Depression Economics," *Foreign Affairs* (January–February 1999).
20. Sato (1988).
21. Pressnell (1973), p. 5.
22. Davies (1994), p. 580.
23. In most industries a high output/worker ratio is a measurement of efficient

use of labor. This is not necessarily so in the banking industry. A high output/ worker ratio may be a measure of recklessness in allocating credit. In Japanese and Chinese banking, such a high asset/labor ratio could be viewed as a confirmation of the abacus approach to bank management.

24. The difference between lending rates and borrowing (deposit) rates.

25. For details, see Mourdoukoutas (1993), ch. 3.

26. Horvat (1998).

27. Sapsford (1998), p. A3.

28. Hartcher (1998), p. 71.

29. Ibid., p. 135.

30. Doherty (1998a), p. MW11.

31. Ibid., p. MW10.

32. "How the Mighty Are Falling," *Euromoney* (editorial) (September 1998), p. 202.

Part I

The Rise and Fall of Abacus Banking and the Banking Crisis in Japan

Chapter 2

The Rise of
Abacus Banking in Japan

In the summer of 1997, in the middle of the banking crisis, one of the authors tried to wire money to the United States through a major bank in Japan. To his dismay, the employee-crowded branch could not handle the wire transfer and he had to visit another downtown branch, not to mention that he had a hard time finding someone who could speak English. But even when he arrived at the other branch, things were no better. He received several greetings, a box of tissues, and free blood pressure monitoring services, but not the "core" banking services he expected. In fact, it was easier for the Foreign Exchange desk manager at the bank to recommend a "competing" bank rather than undergo the procedure of wire transferring. In the end, after waiting for over an hour and after checking his blood pressure several times in the monitor across the bank counter, the desk manager did him a "favor." He went to an ATM machine to withdraw the cash, counted the money three times—one with his abacus, another with an electronic calculator, and a third in his PC—and wired it to the United States, for a hefty triple fee: a currency conversion fee, a wire transfer fee, and the loss of ten days' interest (the time it took the bank to have the funds transferred).

Though just a personal experience, this example demonstrates how Japanese banks treat their clients, and how such treatment differs from that offered by banks in other countries, especially the United States. Specifically, in the United States, a visit to the local branch of a major bank and a moderate fee are sufficient for wiring money overnight, all over the world. But the difference between Japanese and U.S. and European banking extends beyond money-wiring procedures and fees to the ways that Japanese banking performs its fundamental functions and earns its income, and the ways that government bureaucrats supervise the industry and control the behavior of bank managers.

In the United States, private banks are true for-profit institutions. According to prevailing corporate governance, individual and institutional stockholders who appoint professional managers to oversee the day-to-day operations own them. In this sense, managers are accountable to the bank stockholders. They must enhance stockholder value or risk losing their positions.[1] At the same time, bank managers must limit traditional risks (liquidity and credit risks), market risks (foreign currency risk, interest rate risk, liquidation risk, etc.), and operational risks. Government regulators impose a number of constraints to limit competition in the banking industry and the risks associated with it. The Glass-Steagall Act, for instance, limits cross-state competition and competition between the banking and securities industries. Yet government regulators do not monitor the day-to-day operations of individual banks and control the behavior of bank managers. This has been especially true since the late to mid-1970s, when currency liberalization, financial deregulation, and globalization weakened the Glass-Steagall Act and increased both market opportunities and risks. In this sense, U.S. bank managers perform a dual function—as accountants, monitoring fund flows in and out of the bank treasury, and as credit risk analysts, evaluating the risk and returns of investment alternatives.

In contrast to American banks, Japanese private banks are not true for-profit institutions. According to the prevailing corporate governance, bank stockholders appoint management to oversee day-to-day operations, but have little control over it.[2] Specifically, banks that are owned by large corporations and operate under what is known as *keiretsu* relations are not too concerned with profits, but rather with relations and mutual obligations with other *keiretsu* members. In this form of "relational banking," banks serve more as corporate welfare agencies, providing low-cost financing to their *keiretsu* clients who are also their shareholders as compared to other clients, rather than as true, profit-maximizing enterprises. Japanese banks are not overly concerned with traditional banking risks either. Under a policy known as "overlending," for instance, the BOJ has virtually eliminated liquidity risk.

Keiretsu relations, fast economic growth, and rising asset prices have

also limited individual and systemic credit risk. Tight government regulation has limited competition among banks' corporate clients, among
banks and the securities industries, and among banks themselves, reducing market risks. Government regulation further monitors the day-
to-day performance of banks, controlling, in essence, the behavior of
bank managers. In contrast to their American counterparts, Japanese
bank managers basically perform only one function—that of accountants
or abacus bankers, who keep records of transactions and assign loans
according to government guidelines and *keiretsu* relationships rather than
according to the principles of credit risk management. In this sense, Japanese banks have grown accustomed to deriving their income from a
thin interest rate spread rather than through investment risk management. This has been particularly true in the first four decades that followed the Occupation, an era of high economic growth and savings rates,
tight government regulation, and asset inflation.

Arguing this hypothesis in more detail, this chapter takes a closer look
at a number of structural facets of the "extended high-growth" era, from
the early 1950s to the late 1980s, and investigates how such facets nurtured abacus banking.[3] Specifically, the chapter reviews the sources of
Japan's economic growth, business relations, and government policies
over the said period, and how they have provided a virtually risk-free
environment, giving rise to abacus banking.

Japan's postwar economic expansion began with the economic reforms
of the Occupation, especially the breaking of *zaibatsu* groups, land reform, and democratization of the political system:

Probably the most important among the reform programs were land reforms and
the revision of the constitution, both of which have a lasting impact on Japanese
society, most likely because they found solid backing in the minds of Japanese
people themselves.[4]

Occupation's economic reforms were supplemented by post-Occupation
government policies, which included the importation of foreign technology, the protection of domestic industry, U.S. investment and instant
access of Japanese corporations to the American market, and macroeconomic stability.[5]

In addition to Occupation reforms and post-Occupation government
policies, a number of demand and supply factors have contributed to
Japan's economic growth. On the demand side, domestic demand
growth played a major role in accommodating economies of scale and

sparking growth in the 1950s and 1960s. According to Denison and Chung's classic study on the sources of growth, a major factor in Japan's growth for the period 1950–1962 has been the economies of scale, a much more important factor than in other industrialized countries.[6] A study by Porter further supports this point:

Demand conditions proved to be one of the most important of the determinants of national competitive advantage in Japanese industry. In a remarkable number of industries in which Japan achieved strong positions, the nature of domestic demand characteristics provided a unique stimulus to Japanese companies. The domestic market, not the foreign markets, led industry development in the vast majority of Japanese industries. Only later did exports become significant.[7]

Exports played a role in the 1950s, but they became important much later—indeed, after the first oil shock, and even then the growth of exports lasted for only ten years, until 1985, when the yen appreciation forced Japan to switch to domestic demand growth.[8] Export demand grew at 17 percent in 1976, 12 percent in 1977, 18 percent in 1980, and 14 percent in 1981; exports declined by 1.4 percent in 1986, 1 percent in 1987, and 0.5 percent in 1990, and they remained stagnant throughout the mid-1990s. Domestic demand rose by 4.1 percent, 6.2 percent, and 4.6 percent for the corresponding years, and although at low rates, demand picked up in the early to mid-1990s.[9]

On the supply side, growth in inputs, that is to say, growth in the labor force and in labor force participation, expansion of working hours, gains in labor productivity, and growth in total factor productivity (spread of new technology) account for Japan's rapid economic growth. In fact, employment rose at an annual rate of 1.3 percent between 1960 and 1973, 0.6 percent between 1973 and 1979, and 1.2 percent between 1979 and 1989. Between 1979 and 1988, labor productivity increased at 3.1 percent, compared to 0.9 percent for the United States and 1.9 percent for Germany; between 1989 and 1993, labor productivity increased by 1.4 percent in Japan, compared to 1.5 percent for the United States and 0.3 percent for Germany. Between 1979 and 1988, total factor productivity increased at a rate of 1.8 percent, well above the corresponding rates of 0.4 percent for the United States and 0.7 percent for Germany; between 1988 and 1993, total factor productivity in the United States increased by 2.4 percent in Japan, compared to 2.3 percent in the United States and 0.1 percent in Germany. Overall, for the period 1979–1995, Japan's total factor productivity increased by 1.2 percent annually, compared to 0.5

Exhibit 2.1
Economic Plans: Fiscal Years, GNP Growth Target, and Average Annual GNP Growth Achieved (1956–1992)

Years	Target	Achieved	Key Goals
1956–1960	4.9	8.8	Economic self-reliance, full employment
1958–1962	6.5	9.7	Maximum growth, full employment, higher standard of living
1961–1970	7.8	10.0	Same as above
1964–1968	8.1	10.1	Correction of higher growth problem
1967–1971	8.2	9.8	Balanced development
1970–1975	10.6	5.1	A more comfortable Japan
1973–1977	9.4	3.5	Improved social welfare, international cooperation
1976–1980	6.0	4.5	Stable development
1979–1985	5.7	3.9	Stable growth, increase in quality of life, contributions to international welfare
1983–1990	4.0	4.5	Promotion of international stability, more vitality in economy and society
1988–1992	3.7	5.4	Reduction of external imbalances, society where people can "feel" affluence

percent for the United States and 0.4 for Germany. It is these gains in total factor productivity, a kind of technological catch-up, that have pushed Japan well past the limitations of input growth.[10]

In most Western societies, policy makers are preoccupied with consumer prosperity, but not in Japan. In this country, production comes before consumption, work before leisure, and corporation before family, at least in the first three decades that followed the end of the Occupation. "Grow or perish"—that is how the "Yoshida Doctrine" defined Japan's economic strategy in the postwar era. Reflecting this doctrine, all three economic plans from 1958 to 1970 stated explicitly that maximum growth was the most important goal (see Exhibit 2.1). The Income Doubling Plan of 1959, for instance, called for high savings and investments as the vehicles to achieving rapid technological innovations and high growth, as did the 1958–1962 plan.

Pursuing the objectives of the Yoshida Doctrine, corporations, workers, banks, and the government all joined forces to accomplish this objective. Companies invested heavily in capital equipment, paid little in divi-

Exhibit 2.2
Real GNP Annual Growth in Major Industrial Countries (1960–1987)

Country	1960–1973	1974–1979	1980–1982	1983–1987
Japan	6.3	3.6	3.7	4.0
United States	2.5	2.6	−0.3	4.0
OECD	4.8	2.9	1.0	3.4

Sources: The Europa World Year Book 1992/94 (London: Europa Publications); OECD (1994a); and IMF (1980).

dends, and emphasized sales and market share growth. Throughout the 1960s and the 1970s, for instance, gross domestic investment accounted for 30–40 percent of GDP, compared to 13–18 percent in the United States.[11] In 1990, Japanese companies had a payout ratio (the proportion of earnings paid out as dividends) of 30 percent, compared to 54 percent for U.S. companies and 66 percent for British companies.[12] At the same time, companies developed close ties with enterprise unions that promoted worker participation, training, joint consultation, flexible compensation, and decision by consensus. For their part, workers demonstrated discipline and cooperation, worked long hours, and saved a great deal. In the mid-1980s, Japanese employees worked 15–20 percent more than their American counterparts, and 25–30 percent more than their Western European counterparts.

By the early 1980s, the objectives of the Yoshida Doctrine had been achieved and even surpassed, and Japan had grown and flourished. For the periods 1956–1960 and 1958–1962, Japan's economy grew at 8.8 percent and 9.7 percent, well above the corresponding 4.9 percent and 6.5 percent target levels (see Exhibit 2.2). For the period 1960–1973, the Japanese economy grew at a rate of 6.3 percent, compared to the 2.5 percent and 4.8 percent corresponding U.S. and OECD (Office of Economic Cooperation and Development) growth rates. For the period 1974–1979, Japan's economy grew at a slower rate of 3.6 percent, but again, above the U.S. and OECD growth averages of 2.6 percent and 2.9 percent. Japan's superior performance continued for the periods 1980–1982 and 1983–1987.

Though eventually services caught up and even surpassed manufacturing, for the most part the said period growth was manufacturing oriented. Even as late as 1989, the service sector provided for 55.8 percent of the GDP and 59 percent of employment; the corresponding figures for the United States were 68.8 percent and 72.5 percent. The industrial sector provided for 41.9 percent of the GDP and 34.6 percent of employment; the corresponding figures for the United States are 29.2 percent, and 24.6 percent, respectively.

High GDP growth rates, accompanied by low inflation and unemployment, have allowed Japanese consumers to enjoy rapid growth in their real income. For the period 1950–1990, real incomes rose from $1,230 (in 1990 prices) to $23,970 (a 7.7 percent average annual growth rate), well ahead of the 1.9 percent growth of the United States, and 1.0 percent of Great Britain.[13] High economic growth rates, low unemployment, and a high per capita GDP placed Japan next to developed nations.

Japan's preoccupation and success with high manufacturing-oriented economic growth provided the country's banks with lending opportunities and a risk cushion, for a number of reasons. First, as discussed earlier, high economic growth was associated with steady employment and rising personal income and savings.[14] With the exception of the years 1981 and 1982, disposable income rose steadily throughout the period 1975–1988, especially in the late 1970s and the late 1980s, when real disposable income rose in excess to 5 percent. Over the same period, savings were close to 20 percent of disposable income.[15] In 1985, Japan's savings accounted for 18 percent of disposable income, compared to Canada's 9.7 percent, France's 12.6 percent, and the United States's 4.9 percent.[16] High savings, in turn, provided a steady supply of deposit funds to banks, especially in the absence of well-developed securities markets.

Every single working day, Japanese individuals and corporations generate over a billion of dollars' worth of savings. This excess cash rushes into domestic bank accounts, stocks, insurance premiums, and real estate speculation, but even these institutions cannot hold it all. Like water seeking its own level, a large amount of it *must* flow abroad.[17]

For the period 1954–1988, for instance, Japan's financial intermediation ratio increased fourfold, while the corresponding U.S. ratio merely doubled (see Exhibit 2.3). For the same period, Japan's indirect financial ratio remained at around 0.70, above the corresponding U.S. ratio (see Exhibit 2.4). For the period 1960–1990, bank deposits stayed high, close to 70 percent of banks' liabilities (see Exhibit 2.5).

A steady supply of deposits, in turn, allowed banks to keep their lending rates low, a factor that is often quoted as a source of competitive

Exhibit 2.3

Asset Accumulation and Financial Intermediation in Japan and the United States (1954–1988)

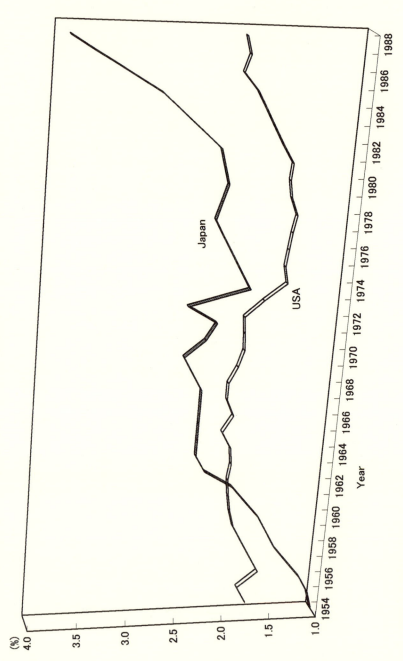

Source: OECD (1990/1991), p. 77.

Exhibit 2.4
Indirect Financing Ratio (1954–1988)

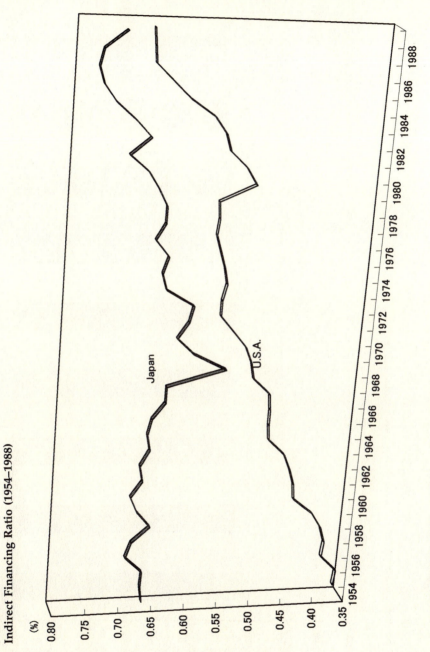

Source: OECD (1990/1991), p. 77.

27

Exhibit 2.5
Bank Deposits in Japan (1960–1996) (percent of total assets)

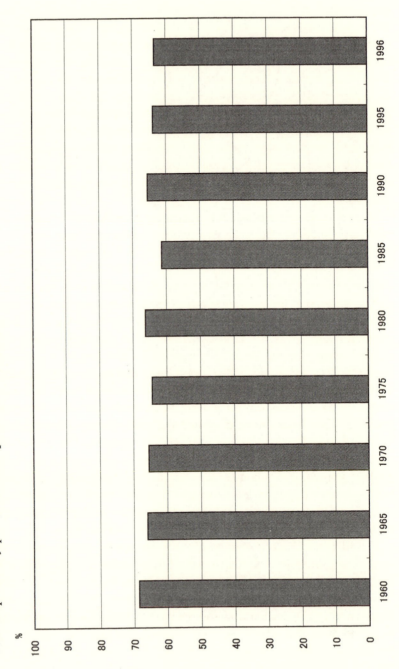

advantage of the Japanese corporations against their American counterparts in the said period.[18] "For Americans operating in many parts of
the world, the biggest problem in competing with the Japanese is not
price but the favorable financing terms that Japanese companies can offer
as a result of their low cost of capital and government guarantees."[19]
Indeed, according to economists Cauly and Zimmer, the cost of capital
for a firm with factories with an average life of 40 years was 5 percent
in 1988 in Japan, compared to 10 percent in the United States, 8 percent
in the United Kingdom, and 5 percent in the former West Germany.[20] In
fact, Japanese lending was so low in the late 1980s that the spread between lending rates and deposit rates was negative, which (as will be
discussed in Chapter 4) is the root cause of the precipitation of the banking crisis.

Second, high growth and low financing rates fueled corporate investment and therefore created a steady demand for corporate loans. For the
period 1980–1990, for instance, bank loans in Japan almost quadrupled,
while U.S. bank loans merely doubled (see Exhibits 2.6 and 2.7). The
demand for corporate loans was particularly strong over the period under consideration for another reason—the lack of direct financial markets
where a corporation could issue equity, as had been the case in other
countries, especially the United States. "Loan demand persistently exceeded supply in the bank loan market in that period, and especially
major banks such as city banks faced huge demands for their loans and
couldn't meet all of them."[21] In this way, Japanese corporations have
relied on bank financing for their capital needs rather on securities financing. "The banks have provided the bulk of corporate sector's borrowing needs. During the 'high-growth' era (prior to the first oil shock)
the domestic capital market was underdeveloped—neither corporations
nor the government relied on it for finance."[22] Specifically, in 1975, corporate borrowing from banks ranged from 43 percent for large corporations to 46 percent for medium corporations and remained high in
1989, an issue that will be further addressed in Chapter 4.

In addition to high economic growth, the ability of Japanese banks to
extend corporate loans almost indefinitely is further reinforced by a long-
standing policy of the BOJ to provide liquidity to banks. Known as
"overborrowing" or "overlending," such policy "chronically extended
more credit, either by lending and/or by purchase of securities, than they
acquired from deposits or their own capital. The gap was filled primarily
by relying on borrowings from the BOJ."[23] This means that the BOJ vir-

Exhibit 2.6
Bank Loans in Japan (1960–1996) (percent of total assets)

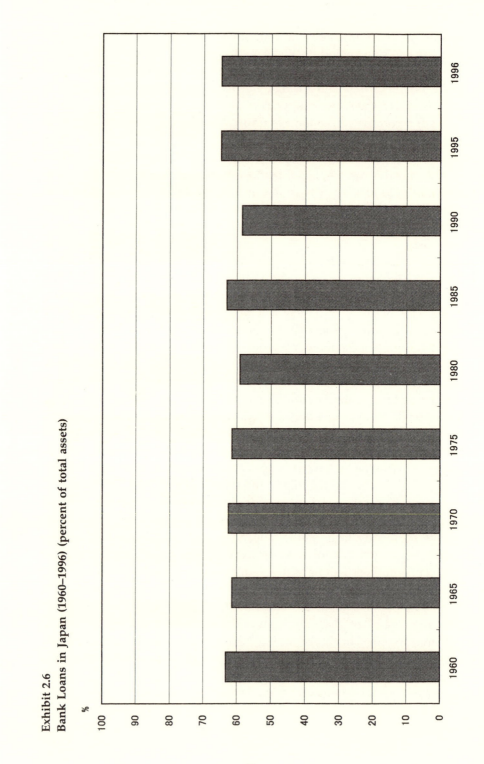

30

Exhibit 2.7
Bank Loans in the United States (1980–1995) (percent of total assets)

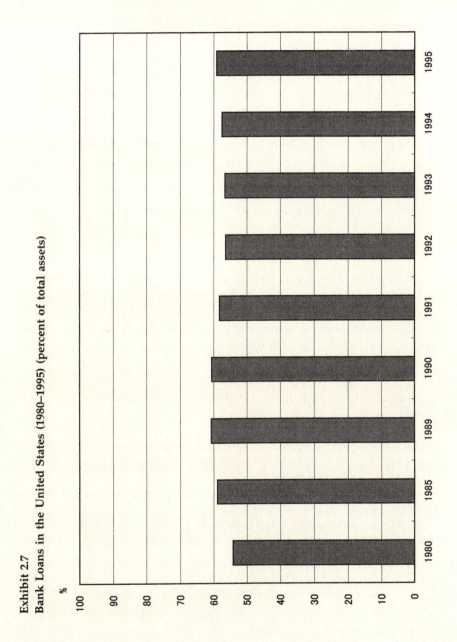

tually eliminated liquidity risk, a traditional banking risk. Adams and Hoshii note:

Due to the readiness of the Bank of Japan to give credit to the commercial banks, liquidity is of practical significance in Japanese banking lending. Hence, the financial managers of the country permitted the so-called overloan situation not only to arise but to continue for long periods without fear of panic or insolvency.[24]

The BOJ policy of overlending can be traced back to the turn of the century, as a vehicle of financing the country's industrialization.

In expanding their loan business, the most powerful banks were able to borrow at special rates from the Bank of Japan, while smaller banks borrowed from the major banks. Through borrowing from the Bank of Japan, the commercial banks were enabled to make loans to industrial enterprises at levels well above those permitted by their own liabilities.[25]

At any rate, permitting "overloan" to continue for long periods, the Japanese private banking system as a whole enjoyed seigniorage income, (i.e., just by creating money). In this sense, "overloan" is both a cause and a consequence of Japan's high economic growth. It is also a cause and a consequence of government regulation of financial markets and close relations between banks and business firms.

Over-loans of commercial banks are fundamentally a result of the high growth rate of the Japanese economy. In post-war Japan, business firms have invested at a rapid rate, so that their demand for funds has been extremely strong. In spite of this development, the capital market has lagged, so that business firms have had to procure funds by borrowing from commercial banks. Under these circumstances, close relationships have tended to develop between commercial banks and business firms. Thus banks have been willing to meet this demand for funds, and in consequence they have been chronically short of cash and liquid reserves. The cash deficiency has been made good by borrowing from the BOJ or from the call money market.[26]

Third, high economic growth and successful overseas expansion created a steady flow of revenue, earnings, and cash flow for Japan's large corporations, especially in the late 1980s. The profit-sales ratio increased steadily from nearly 5 percent in 1984 to nearly 7 percent by 1989, while the net rate of return on corporate assets increased from nearly 0 percent in 1983 to nearly 15 percent in 1989.[27] Over the same period, cash flow increased from 4 percent to nearly to 6 percent.[28] Steady earnings and cash flow in turn allowed Japanese corporations to repay loans to banks.

Fourth, high economic growth was accompanied by asset inflation, especially land inflation in the major city areas. Between 1955 and 1989, land prices at the national level rose sixteenfold, while land prices in the six major city areas rose almost thirtyfold.[29] To be more specific, land price inflation was not just the result of economic growth but also the result of urbanization and population density, tax law, and strict zoning laws that acted as price supports.[30] Equity price rises were as dramatic, especially in the bubble years. Between 1985 and 1989, for instance, Tokyo share prices and land prices in the six major cities rose by 180 percent.[31] In either case, as stocks and land in particular are used as loan collateral, higher prices expand the lending opportunities of banks). Wood States:

So a rising stock market literally increases banks' ability to lend. It also increases the net worth of the corporate sector because of the still widespread system of cross shareholding where companies own shares in one another, not for the purposes of investment but to cement long-standing business relationships.[32]

Higher land and equity prices further provide another credit risk cushion for Japanese banks, in case a loan recipient does not generate sufficient cash value to repay its loans. "In the rare event a borrower went under, his land collateral was as good as gold anyway since legions of land-use restrictions acted as virtual government price supports."[33] Simply put, as long as the assets in collateral are rising in price, banks have little to be concerned about the quality of such assets.

Fifth, as economic growth in the 1950s and the 1960s was concentrated in manufacturing, bank lending was extended to large corporations with tangible assets placed as a collateral, an important requirement for Japanese lending:[34]

Most of the important types of financial transaction in Japan, including corporate debenture issue, bank lending, and interbank transactions, require the provision of collateral. This practice is unique to Japan; in the other industrialized countries, the provision of the collateral is decided on a case-by-case basis between the parties to the transaction, and, in fact, there are many cases in which collateral is required.[35]

This means that Japanese bankers did not make a special effort to appraise and assess the value of well-known companies with highly visible products and assets, especially as long as both sales and asset prices grew exponentially. Simply put, Japanese bankers did not have to possess any special skills or apply any advanced risk management techniques to evaluate the creditworthiness of loan applicants; the use of an abacus calculator was sufficient. Besides, a steady, long-term economic growth allowed Japanese banks to conceal losses in bad years and make up for them in good years.

In short, "overlending," robust, manufacturing-oriented economic growth, high savings, and asset inflation allowed the Japanese banking system as a whole to enjoy seigniorage income, limiting its exposure to traditional banking risks at the same time. As long as the BOJ provided sufficient liquidity, as long as the economy grew, as long as savings continued to pour into the banking system, and as long as assets placed for collateral were tangible and rising in value, Japanese bank managers did not have to be concerned with traditional banking risks. But Japanese managers did not have to be concerned about risk for another, fundamental reason. In a country where business-to-business and business-to-government relations come before profit, individual risk becomes irrelevant in evaluating creditworthiness and managing bank portfolios.

To be fair, business-to-business relations are an important factor in the evaluation of prospective clients' creditworthiness in every country around the world. Yet in most developed countries, to avoid market concentration and control, government regulation separates bank governance from corporate governance. Banks cannot be major shareholders of corporations, and corporations cannot be the major stockholders of banks (i.e., corporate directors do not sit on the boards of banks, and bank directors cannot sit on the boards of corporations). In the United States, for instance, banking and anti-trust regulation prohibits banks from holding equity positions. Anti-trust regulation further limits cross-corporate holdings.

The separation of bank governance from corporate governance allows corporations and banks to pursue independently the interests of their own stockholders; the interests of bank shareholders and the interests of the shareholders of their corporate clients may be in conflict with each other. Higher lending rates, for instance, may benefit the bank shareholders, but they may hurt the shareholders of their corporate clients. Banks may further decide to scale back credit to customers whose creditworthiness has diminished, due, for example, to deterioration in their economic or financial situation. In addition, in most countries around the world, management is accountable to its stockholders, and strict disclosure laws allow the general public to evaluate banks as depository and investment institutions.

In Japan, the important factor in evaluating prospective clients and extending credit to them is business-to-business relations, especially relations between banks and their clients, often supported by long-lasting cross-ownership holdings.[36]

Increasingly, business relations among companies, be they industrial or financial, became cemented by cross-shareholding arrangements. Over time, an intricate web of cross-holding emerged. By 1955, cross-shareholding was at 25 percent of outstanding stocks listed on the Tokyo Stock Exchange and, by 1960, at about 40 percent.[37]

In 1988, banks held 17 percent of the Tokyo Stock Exchange's listed shares, while corporations held 44 percent of the bank-listed shares.[38] A 1995 OECD survey further finds that in Japan, banks owned 26.7 percent of stocks, compared to 0.3 percent in the United States, 12 percent in Germany, 4.3 percent in France, and 0.9 in the United Kingdom.[39]

Combined with an implicit commitment of the large corporations to enterprise unions to warrant lifetime employment to their regular employees, cross-ownership holdings make it more convenient, even mandatory, for banks to focus on a strategy of money creation—low-interest volume lending. Low-interest volume lending allows *keiretsu* members to aggressively expand their sales and market shares to provide stable employment and high wages for their employees.[40] In this way, banks pursue the interests of their stakeholders rather than their stockholders, a practice that can be traced back to the National Mobilization Law, introduced in the late 1930s, as a way of promoting social peace between labor and management.[41] According to Noguchi,

Before the war, companies primarily pursued the interests of shareholders, and direct financing—obtaining funds through the financial markets—was much more prevalent. That began to change as the nation prepared for war. In 1938 came the national mobilization law, which restricted shareholders' rights and prompted companies to place priority on keeping workers happy. This was designed to instill a sense of belonging and security, thus contributing to worker productivity.[42]

Relations between banks and their corporate clients could be described as " 'a system of corporate financing and governance,' by emphasizing the reciprocal delegation of monitoring among banks and the subordination arrangement in the event borrowing firms experience financial distress."[43] As a result, commercial banks, in particular city banks, have had very close relationships with their business customers. City banks often serve as "main banks," arranging for syndicated loans to their corporate clients, which by definition diversify the risk exposure of each syndicate bank to a particular corporate loan. As of 1994, for instance, Sakura Bank served as a main bank to 132 firms, Fuji Bank to 132 firms, and Tokai Bank to 100 firms.[44] Each main bank is

committed to stabilize the business performance of a borrowing firm through bank finance and control, while it maintains the right to intervene in the borrowing firm's management. That is, to fulfill the firm's demand for bank loans and to keep loan-risk diversion, the main bank organizes a "de facto" loan consortium by implicitly guaranteeing the creditworthiness of the firm to other non-main banks or by allowing a free-ride for non-main banks in monitoring activities.[45]

At times, relationships between main banks and their business clients are so close that they meddle in one another's business and even corporate governance, which has contributed to overlending.

Dependent for their own success upon the success of the firms of their group, the banks typically found that it made sense both to support and supervise them, and adopted the practice of sending representatives to the members' boards of directors to monitor the firms' activities and to provide information and advice, as well as funds.[46]

A bank too closely linked with a particular business firm may easily be involved in the latter's competition with other groups, so that banks are liable to extend credit too freely; it has to be recognized that this has been a factor making for overlending of the economy.[47]

The melding of governance of corporate and lending institutions is permitted by the absence of sound corporate governance laws, and the lack of disclosure laws in essence turns the MOF into the *de facto* guarantor of the soundness of the banking industry.

Among the industrialized countries, disclosure of a bank's books is one of the most important resources the public has for evaluating a bank as an equity investment or as a reliable depository institution. In Japan, it could be argued, the MOF's implicit guarantee against bank failure is the functional equivalent of full disclosure.[48]

The rather unusual corporate governance further creates a peculiar situation. First, banks serve as corporate welfare institutions rather than as true for-profit institutions. As the leader of the *keiretsu* group, Japanese banks have turned to the financing arm of the corporate members and must be prepared to finance their credit needs, irrespective of the economic situation of each corporate member or the feasibility of the projects pursued. This function of Japanese banks is reflected in the low interest rate spread, often 50 basis points or about 1 percent of the banks assets, compared to 3.8 percent of U.S. banks, 3.6 percent of Italian banks, and 3 percent of U.K. banks.[49] A low interest rate income margin and a low return on equity (ROE) in turn means that Japanese banks collect little, if any, premium for risk. In 1996, for instance, Japanese banks earned a net rate of ROE of 2.1 percent, well below a corresponding 20.7 percent ROE of their U.S. counterparts (see Exhibit 2.8).

The inability of banks to raise lending rates supports and reinforces the policy of overlending and leaves Japanese banks vulnerable in case of loan defaults, an issue that will be addressed in subsequent chapters. Second, *keiretsu* relations serve as another buffer against liquidity risk for Japanese banks. Should a member bank or a finance corporation face liquidity problems, *keiretsu* members often will come to their rescue. Conversely, *keiretsu* relations oblige banks to come to the rescue of inefficient members that the market would have otherwise washed away. Yamaichi Securities and Yasuda Trust are two examples. In 1965, for instance, Fuji and Mitsubishi Bank, in collaboration with the MOF and the BOJ, rescued Yamaichi Corporation, a member of the same *keiretsu* group. In February 1998, Fuji Bank, the main bank for the Fuyo *keiretsu* group, poured in close to $850 million to rescue Yasuda Trust, a member of the same *keiretsu*, while for the period 1978–1985, close to 52 percent of all firms in financial distress were rescued by their "main bank."[50] Third, close *keiretsu* relations and the system of mutual obligations reinforce secrecy, non-disclosure, and *bogai* (i.e., detour the losses in subsidiaries set up for this purpose). *Keiretsu* members are reluctant to reveal the financial difficulties of their members, and they make bank managers accountable to other *keiretsu* members rather than to the stockholders.

Exhibit 2.8
International Comparison of Bank Profitability

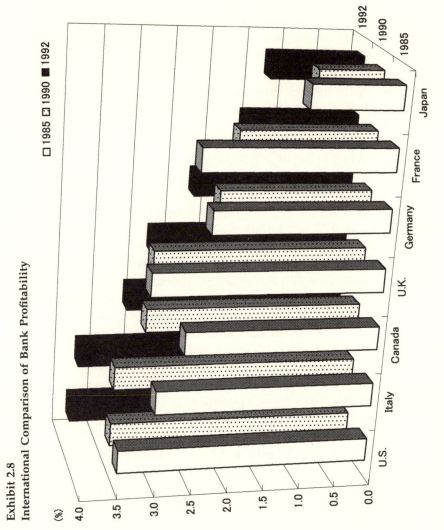

Source: OECD (1995), p. 58.

Besides, as was discussed earlier, in a fast-growing economy, concealing short-term losses in bad years is not a problem; they will be made up in good years.

In short, main bank-centered *keiretsu* relations and loan syndicates associated with it diversify corporate lending and therefore limit credit risk. At the same time, *keiretsu* relations limit the freedom and ability of Japanese bank managers to manage risks (i.e., to allocate credit according to the creditworthiness of their prospective clients). They further reinforce a volume-lending strategy that boosts seigniorage income, a strategy that eventually led to overlending and to the banking crisis, which will be addressed in the following chapters. But what limits the freedom of Japanese bank managers to manage risk the most is their close relations with the government regulators.

Ever since the Meiji Restoration, good relations with bureaucrats were the necessary and often the sufficient condition for pursuing any kind of business in Japan. In the early days of the Restoration, for instance, the Japanese government assisted business to import foreign technology from abroad. In some cases the government even set up model factories, which in turn were handed over to the private sector. In addition, the government provided industrial guidance (i.e., it chose the industries that the private sector should pursue and set up the parameters and incentives to ensure that the private sector would follow through). In this way, each sector of the economy developed

a clientele relation to a ministry or agency of the government. The ministry by statute can wield various sticks and carrots in dealing with the economic sector, but it also holds a general implied administrative responsibility and authority that goes well beyond what is customary in the United States, though it may come close to French practice.[51]

MITI, for instance, formulated "visions" for the future of the Japanese economy and chose to promote the industries that served such visions. The Ministry of Postal Savings in turn allocated the appropriate postal funds to finance the industries pursued. For its part, the mighty MOF issued its own directives to private banks to supplement the financing of the said industries and stood ready to rescue such industries in periods of economic decline. In this way, the Japanese government's intervention in the banking industry extends beyond the conventional regulation, which is the case in other countries. It is an intervention in the daily functioning of banks and corporations, which in essence limits banking risks and controls the behavior of bank managers. According to Adams and Hoshii,

The most important institution in the field of banking and credit, however, is the Ministry of Finance, which shapes fiscal and monetary policies, supervises not only all credit institutions but also the *financial behavior of all corporations*, collects taxes and customs duties, controls foreign exchange, and has a decisive voice in the approval of foreign investment in Japan and Japanese investments overseas.[52] (emphasis added)

The active intervention of government regulators in the economy and the meddling with corporate governance continued well after Japan was transformed to an advanced developed country, until the burst of the bubble economy in the late 1980s, when the government took measures to protect domestic industry from foreign competition and to control foreign currency fluctuations. Specifically, protectionism has taken several forms and faces. In the late 1940s and early 1950s protectionism was in the classical form, the infant industry type. Imports of commodities and resources that would threaten Japan's infant industries were formally restricted. But as the Japanese economy took off and Japanese products captured the world markets, formal import barriers were replaced by informal ones that delayed the pace or even blocked foreign access to many industries until domestic companies developed and flexed sufficient competitive muscle. Take the case of semiconductors, for instance. After failing to promote the domestic computer industry in the mid-1960, MITI introduced stiff trade barriers for foreign companies. Permits for the establishment of foreign subsidiaries and the import of computer microchips were denied, and Japanese executives were even discouraged from working for foreign computer companies.[53]

In addition, MITI continued its pre-war policy, assisting industries in recovering from the economic stagnation that followed the oil and yen shocks. Under the Temporary Act for the Specially Designated Industries, for instance, MITI provided the incentives to persuade companies affected by the oil shock to reduce capacity and transfer resources to new business. MITI has further been instrumental in bringing together corporations for the development of technological applications and coping with the two oil shocks and the yen shock. In this way, "unlike Western governments, which function as regulators of industry, the Japanese bureaucracy serves as a facilitator, an organization dedicated to securing cooperation in keeping economic objectives going smoothly."[54] According to Abegglen, this means that

the government of Japan stands behind the debt position of major Japanese companies, thus both making possible the financing necessary for rapid growth and ensuring that the government through the power of persuasion will play a central role in determining the nature and the direction of that growth.[55]

Standing behind the debt of large corporations, the Japanese government in essence eliminated both traditional and non-traditional banking risks for Japanese banks. But government bureaucrats provided another, perhaps even more effective way of eliminating risks for Japanese banks—tight financial and banking regulation—which, as stated earlier, controlled the behavior of bank managers and made risk management irrelevant altogether.

Specifically, financial regulation eliminated risks for banks by limiting competition both across banking and securities industries and within the banking industry. MOF regulation insulates Japanese banks from outside competition while preventing excessive competition among them. The MOF "extended an unqualified guarantee against failure, promising implicitly to use its full armada of powers to keep banks afloat."[56] Exchange rate controls and restrictions on foreign capital flows limited the entry of foreign banks and securities companies into the Japanese financial markets, eliminating the exchange rate risks. "Restrictions on inward and outward capital flows prevented savers and borrowers from exploiting foreign capital markets, ensuring that domestic credit restraint was not frustrated by capital inflows under the fixed exchange rate system."[57]

The Securities and Exchange Law of 1948, the Japanese version of the Glass-Steagall Act of 1933, limited competition between traditional banking and securities, except for the purchase of securities for their own account. But financial regulation reached beyond industry entry restrictions. It strictly defined the types of business and products to be offered by banks, creating city banks, regional banks, and trust banks and overseeing their day-to-day operations. "In addition to keeping government control of foreign interest rates and preventing the siren song of market forces from luring capital offshore, a rigid segmentation of financial institutions historically worked to keep Japan's flow of funds in a constant steady state."[58]

In some cases, the MOF intervened either alone or with other banks to rescue a failing bank. According to Ikeo,

When, in the past, the government recognized a failing bank, it intervened directly and the bank's operations were restored. If it proved impossible to restore the bank using the bank's own resources the government appealed to other banks and financial institutions, either for assistance or to absorb the failing institution into their own organization.[59]

Japan's tight banking regulation replicates a government cartel, a *Gosou-sendan Houshiki*, an "escorted convoy" system. MOF "destroyers" protect banks from outsiders and ensure that they are all moved in tandem, without crushing one against the other (see Exhibit 2.9). In plain economic terms, government regulation has turned the Japanese banking industry into an oligopoly cartel, where prices are closely controlled. According to Hartcher,

Prices—in the form of interest rates—were closely controlled by the ministry in unofficial but binding consultation with the banks. Even after the banks were legally granted full freedom to decide their own interest rates, they continued to set them in concert at agreed levels. The banks also worked intimately with the ministry deciding the level of services they offered customers and even the salaries they paid their staff.[60]

To preserve this type of cartel-like system, MOF "sanctions are imposed on cartel-breakers by public authorities whose role is to preserve the integrity of the cartel."[61]

One way that the MOF keeps banks moving together is through licensing (i.e., the requirement that banks must submit any new business proposal to the MOF for approval). The MOF approves applications for the establishment of banks, applications for the reductions in bank capital, the opening and closing of branches, and the merger and liquidation of existing bank operations. Once the MOF approves a new business for a bank, it applies it to all banks. The development of *jusen* is a case in point. Within a year after their approval, the MOF convinced banks to enter the market for individual homeowner mortgages, intensifying competition and eliminating market rents for *jusen*. In this sense, banks can compete in one way only, through volume (i.e., through growth of the overall industry), making the pieces of the pie larger by making the pie larger (see Exhibit 2.10). Thus, "a clear distinction between innovating leaders and less innovative followers has been clouded by the Japanese government through a system of administrative licensing and approvals,

Exhibit 2.9
Gosou-sendan Houshiki

City Banks

Regional Banks

Trust Banks

Security Companies
Insurance Companies

Long-term Credit Banks

Exhibit 2.10
Bank Assets, Economic Growth, and *Gosou-sendan Houshiki*

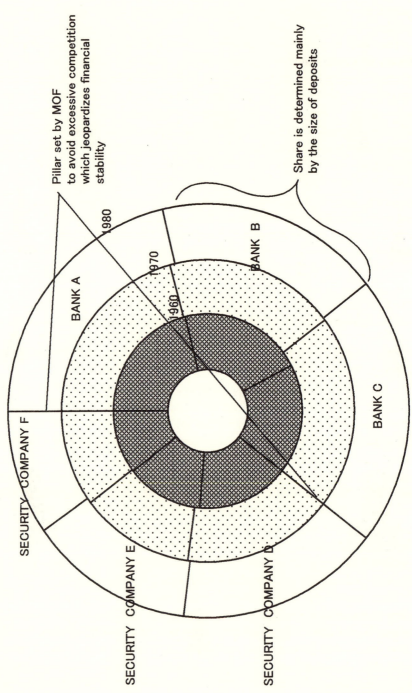
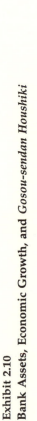

which has generally retarded innovation in the banking industry as a whole."[62]

The MOF further monitors and inspects the day-to-day operations of banks and asks them to restructure their asset and liability positions as deemed appropriate. But once again, the MOF monitors bank operations closely so as to virtually control the behavior of bank managers. For the sake of the "protection of depositors," for instance, MOF officers are allowed to meddle in banks' day-to-day operations, in essence running banks, enjoying benefits that could be viewed as outright bribes in other countries.

Japan's Ministry of Finance is much more than an office of government. It is a political, economic, and intellectual force without parallel in the developed world. It enjoys greater concentration of powers, formal, and informal, than any comparable body in any other industrialized democracy. In Japan, there is no institution with more power.[63]

The minister may also ask banks at any time to submit reports on their business and accounts, and can inspect them. He can order a bank to close or compound its assets in a deposit office, or issue any other orders deemed necessary, should a bank commit illegal acts or the Minister considers that a deterioration in its financial condition necessitates such measures to protect depositors.[64]

With such vested powers and with little checks and balances by the other two constitutional powers (the legislative and the judiciary), the MOF rather than bank managers decided how credit should be allocated, which has resulted in a rather peculiar relationship between the regulators and the regulated. First, the regulated (banks) cooperate with the regulators (the MOF) to conceal non-performing assets, as evidenced in the Daiwa Bank's New York trading losses. Second, the fear of MOF inspections, for instance, has led Japanese banks to devote substantial resources to enjoying good relations with the MOF (this includes the designation of a bank officer, MOF-tan, to entertain MOF inspectors, so the bank can obtain leads about forthcoming inspections).

Third, good relations between banks and the MOF also include the very well-known practice of *amakundori*, or "descent from heaven," where banks offer high-paid positions to former MOF officers. In this way, banks end up managed by former MOF executives, imbued in bureaucracy and immersed in law and government rather than in economics or management. This means that former MOF bureaucrats make bad bank managers. Banks run by former MOF bureaucrats have lower ROEs as compared to banks run by non-MOF bureaucrats. As Hartcher observes: "The independent banks were on average 4.6 percent more profitable than those run by former officials of the central bank, and 7.4 percent more profitable than those headed by former officials of Okurasho."[65] Hartcher attributes this to a lack of expertise.

The Okurasho wants its staff to understand economics but not to be possessed by it. It wants officials who see economics but not to be possessed by it. It wants officials who see economics as one set of considerations and legal principles rather than those of economics as paramount.[66]

The Economist has another explanation:

Technological innovation has left officials trained as generalists unable to grasp many of the issues that they now have to confront. Bureaucratic shortcomings occur in all countries, but in Japan officials assume wide-ranging powers for the kind of detailed policymaking that is done by expert groups in countries elsewhere.[67]

Fourth, under these circumstances, according to Ikeo,

Bank managers cannot be completely responsible for their actions. When a bank runs into a difficult situation, it becomes nearly impossible to determine whether the situation is the result of bad decision-making on the part of the bank's management or improper guidance on the part of bank regulators.[68]

In addition, banks had little incentive to assume risks in developing new products. As Ikeo puts it, "The convoy system of administrative guidance is incompatible with innovation simply because innovation implies cartel destruction."[69]

In short, Japanese banks have neither the freedom nor the expertise to function as true for-profit banking institutions. Though by and large privately owned, the Japanese banking sector resembles more the banking of a centrally planned economy rather than that of the market economies, most notably the United States.[70] Credit is rationed under government guidance and the close ties between borrowers and lenders rather than under a credit risk management regime.

At this point, one should raise two questions. First, if in a sense tight government regulation creates an economic environment similar to that of centrally planned economies, how did a number of Japanese manufacturing industries succeed to compete in world markets? Second, why have Japan's trade partners, especially the United States, tolerated such practices?

In answering the first question, economists divide the Japanese economy into two sectors—a modern, export-oriented sector and a backward domestic sector, arguing that it is the modern, export-oriented sector that succeeded in world markets.[71] Economists further argue that this sector succeeded not because of but in spite of government regulation. According to Porter,

In a number of industries, the government erroneously attempted to limit the number of Japanese competitors. Examples include steel, autos, machine tools, and computers. The unwillingness of Japanese companies to abide by government consolidation plans proved to be a blessing, and intense domestic rivalry contributed to international success. In the 1980s, MITI has become more aware of the importance of domestic rivalry, though the tendency to limit competition is a continuing problem.[72]

While the *zaibatsu* structure concentrated economic power in prewar Japan, its breakup by the allies unleashed a level of competition that is unmatched in any nation. Virtually every significant industry in which Japan has achieved an international competitive advantage is populated by several and often a dozen or more competitors.[73]

In spite of protectionism, rivalry and competition were maintained in many industries, especially those that had been successful in the world markets. The number of competitors ranges from 4 in motorcycles and musical instruments to 25 in audio equipment and 112 in machine tools. Thus, unlike European industrial policies, which use protectionism to restrict competition, Japan's industrial policies use protectionism to strengthen competition, in targeted sectors.

The answer to the second question, that is, why Japan's trade partners, especially the United States, have tolerated such practices, is twofold. First, as argued elsewhere, counting on Japan as an indispensable ally in containing Soviet and Chinese expansion in the Asian-Pacific region, the United States awarded Japan a generous "dowry"[74]—GATT/IMF membership[75] without substantial reciprocation from Japan. Japanese banks could have it both ways, open markets abroad and a sanctuary home, which could explain the rapid overseas expansion of Japanese banks in the late 1970s and the 1980s, which will be addressed in the next chapter.

Second, a substantial part of Japan's banking liquid assets was invested in dollars, allowing the United States to enjoy its own seigniorage (i.e., the United States enjoyed Japanese goods simply by printing money).

To sum up, faced with a fast-growing economy, rising savings and asset values, and with the BOJ prepared to provide sufficient liquidity, Japanese banks had little to be concerned with traditional banking risks in the extended high-growth era. In addition, in this era, traditional banking risks were irrelevant in bank management altogether. Participating in lending consortia arranged by main banks rather than selecting borrowers individually, banks diversified credit risks. As members of *keiretsu* groups and within the *Gosou-sendan Houshiki* (the "escorted convoy" system), bank managers had little freedom to manage bank portfolios in a "rational" way (i.e., in a way that allocated credit according to the principles of profit maximization and credit risk management). Instead, bank managers allotted credit to corporate clients according to *keiretsu* relations and government guidance, a strategy that eventually ran into several snags as soon as the *Gosou-sendan Houshiki* began to disband and the economy began to slow down.

NOTES

1. Indeed, underperforming U.S. corporations are subject to corporate takeovers and stockholder class action suits that may eventually cost managers their jobs.

2. Individual stockholders have no power in Japan. Stockholder meetings are held in name only, and hostile takeovers and class action suits are still unknown in the Japanese corporate world.

3. Strictly speaking, the high growth era ends in 1973 with the first oil shock. But since the Japanese economy resumed its growth two years later, until 1989, we take that as the year the high growth era ended.

4. Tsuru (1993).

5. Kunio (1979).

6. See Fagerberg (1994), table 1. See also Yanagihara (1994).

7. M. Porter, *The Competitive Advantage of Nations* (New York: The Free Press, 1990), p. 280.

8. The Korean War had a strong positive impact on the cotton and steel industries.

9. OECD, *Economic Outlook* (Paris: OECD), various issues.

10. Fagerberg (1994).

11. OECD, *Economic Outlook*, various issues.

12. Morita (1992).

13. "From Miracle to Mid-Life Crisis" (1993).

14. Japan's high-growth era further coincided with favorable demographics that gave another boost to savings, a host of generation cohorts that reached middle age in the 1970s and the 1980s, which in turn boosted savings, adding more fuel to the steady flow of deposit funds into the banking system. Indeed, for decades, Japan had one of the highest savings rates in the industrial world, which in the absence of accessible financial markets ends up in the hands of bankers and in loans to Japanese corporations.

15. OECD (1993), p. 22.

16. Ibid.

17. Burstein (1988), pp. 36–37.

18. "Interest rate spread" is the difference between deposit interest rates and lending interest rates.

19. Burstein (1988), p. 150.

20. Cauly and Zimmer, "Credit Rating in Large Banks," *Quarterly Review of the Federal Reserve Bank of New York* (Summer 1989), pp. 897–922.

21. Shikano (1998), p. 9.

22. OECD, *Economic Outlook* (Paris: OECD, 1990/1991), p. 78.

23. Suzuki (1987), p. 22.

24. Adams and Hoshii (1972), p. 127.

25. Lazonick and O'Sullivan (1997), p. 120.

26. Pressnell (1973), p. 132.

27. Net rate of return equal to rate of return minus long-term interest rates. For details, see OECD (1996), p. 18.

28. OECD (1995), p. 8.

29. OECD (1994b), p. 85.

30. For a detailed discussion, see OECD (1994b), section IV.

31. OECD *Economic Outlook* (1990/1991), p. 77.

32. C. Wood, *The End of Japan Incorporated* (New York: Simon and Schuster, 1994), p. 119.

33. N. Weinberg, "Opiate of the Masses," *Forbes*, November 16, 1998, p. 202.

34. This requirement can be traced back to the late 1920s, but it was gradually abandoned in the early 1980s.

35. Suzuki (1987), p. 43.

36. In this sense, Japan's banking system is similar to that of Germany's, where banks are allowed to hold equity positions and are active in corporate governance.

37. Lazonick and O'Sullivan (1997), p. 125.

38. "Stock Sales Cut into Cross-Holdings," *Nikkei Weekly*, January 11, 1997 (editorial), p. 11.

39. OECD, *Economic Surveys (US)* (Paris: OECD, 1996), p. 127.

40. For details, see Mourdoukoutas (1993), ch. 3.

41. Unable to draw direct financing, companies had to appeal to the banks,

which played the role of both corporate creditors and stockholders. They provide for loans and have a substantial ownership in corporations; each bank is allowed to own up to 5 percent of the stock of a particular corporation. This way, a large part of the stock of a corporation may be in the hands of just a few banks. According to a report by the National Conference of Stock Exchanges in 1986, city and trust banks accounted for 18.9 percent of all stocks publicly held in Japan.

42. Y. Noguchi, "Wartime System Still Has Impact on Economy," *Nikkei Weekly*, January 16, 1995.

43. Ibid., p. 80.

44. Shikano (1998), p. 83.

45. Ibid., p. 81.

46. R. Brenner, "The Economics of Global Turbulance," *New Left Review*, No. 229 (May–June 1998).

47. Pressnell (1973), p. 167.

48. Rosenbluth (1989), p. 112.

49. OECD (1995), p. 58.

50. Shikano (1998), p. 87.

51. H. Patrick and H. Rosovsky (eds.), *Asia's New Giant: How the Japanese Economy Works* (Washington, DC: Brookings Institution, 1976), p. 487.

52. Adams and Hoshii (1972), p. 91.

53. Flamm (1991).

54. Kunio (1979), p. 25.

55. J. Abegglen, *Business Strategies for Japan* (Tokyo: Sophia University, 1970), p. 5.

56. Hartcher (1998), p. 136.

57. OECD, *Economic Outlook* (1990/1991), p. 78.

58. Burstein (1988), p. 118.

59. Ikeo (1999), p. 59.

60. Hartcher (1998), p. 136.

61. Ibid., p. 57.

62. Ibid., p. 57.

63. Hartcher (1998), p. 2.

64. Pressnell (1973), p. 198.

65. Hartcher (1998), p. 41.

66. Ibid., p. 16.

67. "The Japan Puzzle" (1998), p. 23.

68. Ikeo (1999), p. 59.

69. Ibid., p. 57.

70. It comes as no surprise, therefore, that when it comes to regulation, Japan ranks 35th, even behind Russia, with 30 percent of its economy controlled by bureaucracy, compared to 7 percent in the United States. For further discussion, see "The Japan Puzzle" (1998), p. 23.

71. See Mourdoukoutas (1993).
72. Porter (1990), p. 414.
73. Ibid., p. 424.
74. For details, see Arayama and Mourdoukoutas (1999).
75. General Agreement on Tariffs and Trade/International Monetary Fund.

Chapter 3

The Fall of
Abacus Banking in Japan

Cyclical factors and the collapse of the "bubble" economy have played a major role in the current economic situation, but extensive structural changes to Japan's economy, including the hollowing out of domestic industries, internal and external pricing disparities, diminished entrepreneurship in pioneering new sectors, and stagnant technological development, should also be noted.

— Ryutaro Hashimoto, Former Minister of
International Trade and Industry[1]

In the 19th century, under pressure from the United States and other countries to end her national seclusion, Japan totally rebuilt her political, social and economic systems. After World War II, Japan again transformed herself dramatically. Now our country is working to achieve a metamorphosis. The force of global competition leaves us little time to accomplish this task.

— Shoichiro Toyoda, Former CEO,
Toyota Motor Company[2]

Few countries have been lucky in their bid for industrialization, and Japan is one of them. In the last quarter of the nineteenth century, the silkworm disease in Europe provided the country with the opportunity to expand her silk exports and textile industries, earning the proceeds for the imports of much-needed capital goods. In addition, her victory in the Sino-Japanese war and the Shimonoseki Treaty provided Japanese companies with access to China's economic resource and product markets (especially in the market for silk-yarn, a raw material in the textile industry) and a new colony, Taiwan. Through inexpensive yearn imports from China and technology from Europe, Japan managed to transform herself from an exporter of low-value-added agricultural products to high-value-added manufacturing products, eventually challenging Europe and the United States.

In the mid-twentieth century, as an indispensable U.S. ally against the Soviet expansion in Southeast Asia, Japan was rewarded unconditional access to the newly established GATT/IMF regime. Japanese companies could take advantage of an expanding world market without opening her markets to domestic and foreign competition. Once again, through technology imports and exports of manufacturing goods, Japan managed to transform herself from an exporter of labor-intensive products to an exporter of capital intensive products and eventually to an exporter of technology-intensive products.

But as has been the case in the past, Japan's export-led industrialization created tensions with her trade partners, especially the United States. By the 1980s, a soaring trade surplus, aggressive acquisition of U.S. assets, and a growing economic presence in Asia created friction between the two counties. Beginning with President Carter and continuing with President Reagan, America demanded that Japan stimulate her economy and open her markets to foreign products and competition, especially as it became obvious that the Soviet Union was at the verge of collapse and that the United States no longer needed Japan to fight communism in Asia.

Responding to the United States' demands in the early 1980s, Japan eliminated a number of trade and non-trade barriers, especially in industries where domestic corporations had already established a competitive advantage. As part of the 1985 Plaza Accord, for instance, Japan eased up on her monetary policy, lifted tariff and non-tariff trade barriers and government regulations in controversial industries, and allowed the yen to appreciate considerably against the dollar, measures that had a pervasive impact on the country's economy, most notably on the banking industry.

Monetary easing, for instance, created hyperliquidity, which found its way into real estate and equity markets, prompting large corporations to substitute bank financing with debt equity financing. In the meantime,

the lifting of tariff and non-tariff trade barriers and government deregulation intensified both domestic and foreign competition. The introduction of money market and CD accounts in 1985 intensified competition
between banks and mutual fund companies, raising deposit interest
rates. The switching of large corporations (traditionally the largest bank
borrowers) from debt to equity financing and rising deposit rates deliv-
ered a double blow to Japan's banking system and the abacus strategy:
it narrowed the already thin margin between lending and deposit rates,
reducing the volume of lending to corporate clients at the same time.
This was particularly true during the bubble years, when the interest
rate spread turned negative, eliminating one condition of abacus banking.

By the late 1980s, the continuing efforts of Japanese policy makers to
address the country's trade surplus and to avoid a full-scale trade war
with the United States created a new problem, a rise in the cost of living
and an erosion in the country's competitive advantage. The rise in real
estate prices, for instance, made household and business shelter less af-
fordable. Rising wages and a strong yen priced a number of Japanese
products off the world market, prompting the country's major corporations to relocate production offshore; an aging population began to take
its toll on labor supply, savings, and government financing.

To address these problems, Japanese policy makers reversed some of
their earlier policies and accelerated others. In 1990, for instance, to deal
with runaway real estate and equity markets and to curtail rising labor
costs, the BOJ tightened up the money supply. Yielding to foreign and
domestic pressures, Japan continued to deregulate domestic industries.
To address the impact of an aging population on government finances,
policy makers raised taxes twice, in 1993 and in 1996. In the meantime,
the government continued to disband the "escorted convoy" system of
regulation, exposing banks to both external and internal competition.

This new policy shift produced the final blow to the abacus strategy.
With the tightening of both monetary and fiscal policy, economic growth,
corporate profits, and savings and asset values declined. Faced with slow
growth, less regulation, more competition, and declining asset prices,
Japanese banks could no longer survive and prosper merely through
seigniorage income. Instead, they had to search for new sources of income in new, less predictable businesses, a prospect that set the stage
for the decline and fall of abacus banking.

Arguing this proposition, this chapter discusses how international and
domestic pressures prompted Japan to abandon the high-growth, export-

oriented policies of the Yoshida Doctrine for a new, moderate-growth policy that emphasized consumption and symbiosis with trade partners. This chapter further elaborates on how such a policy shift set the Japanese economy on a roller coaster, known as the bubble economy, and its burst, a roller coaster that led to the decline and fall of abacus banking.

As discussed earlier, for decades the United States has been tolerant (and even accommodating) regarding Japan's efforts to expand exports without opening domestic markets to imports and with good reason. First, due to her geographic position, Japan was an indispensable military ally against the Soviet Union and China, especially during the Korean War. Second, Japan's economic development through participation in the newly established GATT/IMF regime was a test case, a demonstration to the rest of Asia and the world that a market system was still a better alternative than communism. Third, with an industry destroyed by the war, the Japanese economy was more of a small, poor partner and less of a large, formidable competitor to the U.S. economy. Fourth, with low per-capita income, high unemployment rates, and a different culture, the domestic Japanese consumer market was too small and too complicated for U.S. corporations.

Japan's special trade arrangements with the United States and the policies that supported and reinforced them created a dual economy—a modern sector and a backward sector.[3] While the modern sector was little regulated and open to domestic and foreign competitors, the backward sector was extensively regulated and insulated from domestic and foreign competition. Construction, for instance, is 100 percent regulated, and so are financial services, electric gas, and mining; some industries, such as railroads and tobacco, remained government-owned monopolies.

Japan's economic dualism in turn created a dual friction, one against her trade partners and another among her citizens. Friction between Japan and her trade partners was centered in three areas. The first was friction over the country's trade and current account surpluses with the United States, which soared from $4 billion and $2 billion respectively in 1970 to $24.3 billion and $16.5 billion respectively by 1979.

[Japan] must also recognize that the present structure of US/Japan economic relations puts US firms at a disadvantage and imposes burdens on the US economy and on the US citizens. The United States cannot accept this indefinitely and will need to respond to prevent harm of its citizens.[4]

The second was friction over the country's aggressive and conspicuous acquisition of highly visible American assets, which the American public found unacceptable. When the Mitsubishi Estate purchased a stake in Rockefeller Center, for instance, major American TV networks introduced the news with images from the bombing of Pearl Harbor. When Fujistu attempted to buy Fairchild Semiconductors in 1987, the U.S. government intervened, and the deal was dropped. In 1989, Congress extended the Exon-Florio amendment that gave the government the power to scrutinize foreign takeovers for national security.

The third was friction over the country's aggressive expansion to Southeast Asia, the world's fastest-growing region at that time.

Friction between Japan and the United States eventually led to several rounds of negotiations, beginning with the Nixon administration over the dumping of textile products in the U.S. market and the growing trade imbalance between the two countries. Negotiations reached a culmination during the 1985 Plaza Accord, which led to Japan's monetary easing and currency appreciation. Between 1985 and 1989, the BOJ cut the official discount rate five times, from 5.5 percent to 2.5 percent, and allowed the yen to appreciate from 0.004 dollar to the yen to 0.007 dollar to the yen (see Exhibit 3.1). The Plaza Accord also included a number of measures for the opening of a controversial sector—the financial sector—to domestic and foreign competition.

- March 1985: Large-denomination money market accounts and certificates of deposit become available; *Euro-yen* lending to non-Japanese residents (lending extended by non-resident banks and foreign branches of Japanese banks) begins.

- April 1985: Yen bankers' acceptance market is inaugurated, decision is made to allow foreign banks to enter trust banking business.

- October 1985: Interest rates on large deposits are liberalized; bond futures markets are established.

- June 1986: Foreign banks are authorized to issue European bonds.

- December 1986: Tokyo offshore market opens.

- November 1987: Domestic commercial paper market opens; *Euro-yen* commercial paper is launched.

- October 1988: Ceiling on share of foreign banks and securities companies as underwriters of government bonds is raised.

- January 1989: New prime rates for short-term loans reflecting market rates are introduced.

- June 1989: Small-unit money market certificates are introduced; Tokyo Financial Futures Exchange opens; *Euro-yen* lending to Japanese residents begins.

Exhibit 3.1
Exchange Rate (1981–1996)

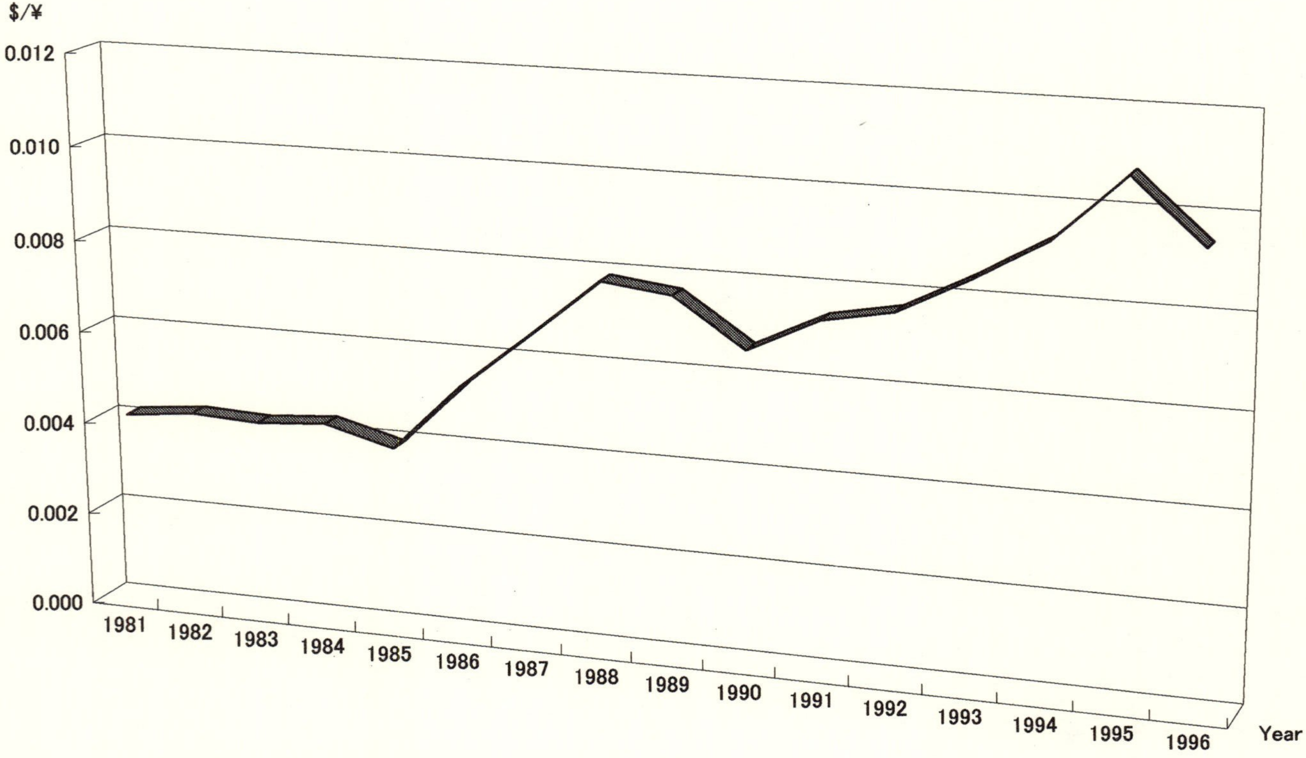

$/¥

Source: Statistics Bureau, Japan Statistical Association (various years).

Efforts to implement these measures had a contradictory impact on the country's banking industry. On the one side, monetary easing and the hyperliquidity that it created accelerated economic growth and asset inflation, strengthening some of the conditions of abacus banking. The GDP, for instance, grew from just below 6 percent in 1986 to over 6 percent by 1988. As reflected in the benchmark Nikkei Index, stock prices rose by 160 percent, from around 14,000 in 1985 to close to 40,000 by 1989. Over the same period, land prices in the Tokyo area more than doubled.

On the other side, hyperliquidity, the rising of equity prices, and a stronger dollar prompted large corporations to issue equity and Euro-bonds instead of borrowing from banks, weakening another condition of abacus banking. Equity offerings increased from 69 in 1986 to 825 by 1990. During the same period, corporate bank borrowing dropped from 21,661 billion yen to 20,889 billion yen.[5] To make things worse for banks, robust economic growth further improved corporate cash flow and allowed large companies to finance their expansion internally. Internal financing increased from 13.8 percent of the overall finance in 1975 to 22.8 percent in 1985 and 26.2 percent in 1989. In the meantime, bank borrowing fell from 43 percent of the total in 1975 to 31.3 percent by 1989 (see Exhibit 3.2).

With large corporations shifting from bank lending to equity and bond offerings, Japanese banks had to shift their lending from the low-risk large corporate clients to the high-risk small and medium corporations. Indeed, bank borrowing of medium-sized firms increased from 46.5 percent of the total in 1975 to 49.5 percent in 1989, while the corresponding figure for small-sized corporations increased from 43.7 percent to 53.6 percent (see Exhibit 3.2).

But what weakened abacus banking the most was financial deregulation, such as the introduction of CDs and other money market instruments, and the liberalization of interest rates on large deposits, which intensified competition between banks and mutual fund corporations, raising interest rate deposits and turning the interest rate spread negative, especially in the period 1987–1990 (see Exhibit 3.3). Competition between banks and non-banks further intensified by raising the ceiling on foreign bank participation in government bond underwriting, the introduction of small-unit money market certificates, and the opening of the Tokyo Financial Futures Exchange.

In short, Japan's efforts to open her markets to foreign products and competition and reduce her trade surplus had a double negative impact

Exhibit 3.2
Financing Ratio of Non-financing Firms (percent, 1975–1989)

		FY1975	1980	1985	1989
Big firms					
Debt		86.2	83.2	77.2	73.8
	Bank borrowing	43.0	38.0	34.8	31.3
	Bond	4.2	5.0	7.5	10.2
Own capital		13.8	16.8	22.8	26.2
Medium-sized firms					
Debt		89.5	88.7	87.3	86.4
	Bank borrowing	46.5	44.7	47.7	49.5
	Bond	0	0.1	0.1	0.3
Own capital		10.5	11.3	12.7	13.6
Small firms					
Debt		87.1	87.3	87.3	86.6
	Bank borrowing	43.7	43.5	48.8	53.6
	Bond	0	0	0	0
Own capital		12.9	12.7	12.7	13.4

Source: OECD (1990/1991), p. 77.

on banks—it lured corporate customers away to equity markets and turned the interest rate spread negative, eliminating two conditions of abacus banking. But as long as the other conditions of abacus banking were in effect (i.e., as long as the economy continued to grow and asset prices to climb, and as long as other government regulations remained intact) abacus banking continued to thrive, but not for very long.

By the late 1980s, Japan's robust economic growth and asset inflation increased the cost of living, especially the extraordinarily high cost of housing, turning Japan into a rich country with poor consumers. In 1991, the size of the average Japanese residence was 881 square feet, compared to 1,645 square feet in the United States, and only 10.3 percent of Japanese homes had central heating and 45.4 percent had flush toilets[6] (the corresponding figures for the United States were 85 percent and 99.8 percent). With such a high cost of living, Japanese people were forced to work long hours, 20–30 percent more than their American and European counterparts. These statistics place Japan closer to less developed rather than to most developed nations:

Exhibit 3.3
Interest Rate Spread (1980–1996)

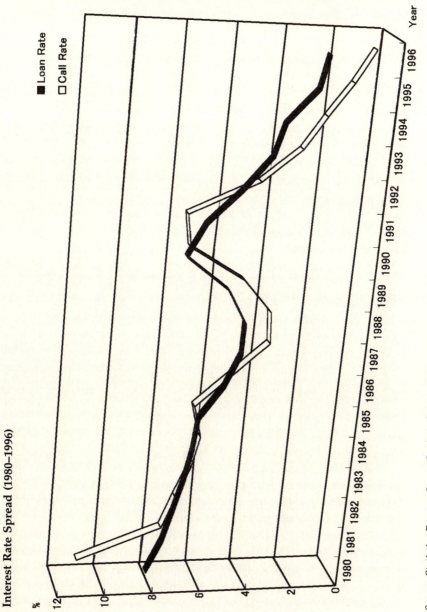

Source: Statistics Bureau, Japan Statistical Association (various years).

Total working hours are recognized internationally as long. In the eyes of many observers, these differences symbolize the failure of workers to share Japan's success. After all, we associate long working hours with poorly developed economies, and short working hours with advanced industrial nations. Japan seems to be an anomaly in this regard.[7]

Compounding the problem of small houses, long working hours, and a high cost of living is a poor infrastructure that lags behind those of other industrialized countries. "In areas ranging from roads to sewer systems to airports, Japan is said to be so far behind her counterparts in the West as not to deserve the label of an advanced developed country."[8] Japan's main sewage system, for instance, serves only 40 percent of the population, compared to 73 percent and 95 percent of the population served by the corresponding U.S. and British sewage systems.[9] In 1990, the average urban Japanese enjoyed 2.2 square meters of park space, compared to 19.2 for the average American living in New York City, 30.4 for the average urban Englishman, and 37.4 for the average urban German.[10]

Japan's rapid rise of asset values, currency appreciation, and economic growth, in conjunction with unfavorable demographics, had another negative impact on the Japanese economy—the erosion of her competitive position. Rapid economic growth, for instance, along with an aging labor force, declining working hours, and tight emigration policies, created severe labor shortages that pushed labor costs higher.[11] Rising labor costs and rising commercial leases, and especially the stronger yen, in turn priced many of Japan's products out of world markets, contributing to "hollowing out," the transfer of traditional manufacturing operations offshore.[12]

Hollowization of the economy is closely related to the movement in exchange rates because the appreciation of the exchange rate will lead to the substitution of imports for domestic production, the substitution of overseas production for domestic production, and the shift in resource allocation from production of tradable goods to production of nontradable goods.[13]

Indeed, the precipitous rise of the yen has made it difficult for Japanese companies, especially consumer electronics companies, to compete effectively in world markets without shifting production in overseas transplants to the United States, the European Union, and especially Asia. In fact, according to some estimates, a 1 percent yen appreciation is followed by a 1.6 percent increase in Japanese investment in Asia.[14] Already, almost 70 percent of the color television sets and about 30 percent of VCRs are made overseas. Japanese companies, like Uniden, the cordless telephone maker, have already relocated their manufacturing outside of Japan.[15] A conformation of this trend is the reduction in Japan's surplus with the United States and an increase in China's and Southeast Asia's surpluses with the United States on the one side and the rise of trade deficits of these countries with Japan on the other side.[16]

"Hollowing out" had two major impacts on the Japanese economy. First, it weakened the traditional *keiretsu* relations, intensifying competition. Second, it fueled a "softomization" of the economy (the growing importance of services over manufacturing), which has contributed to the slowdown of economic growth. In 1995, the service sector provided for 55.8 percent of the GDP and 59 percent of employment; the corresponding figures for the United States were 68.8 percent and 72.5 percent. The industrial sector provided for 41.9 percent of the GDP and 34.6 percent of employment; the corresponding figures for the United States were 29.2 percent and 24.6 percent (see Exhibit 3.4).

As discussed earlier, Japan is further beset by demographic problems arising from the aging of the country's population, which has contributed to the country's labor shortage and has further challenged the country's three major labor institutions (lifetime employment, seniority wages, and enterprise unionism) and has strained Japan's government finance, turning her fiscal surplus into deficit. In this sense, the country found herself in a situation where it criticized her trade partners, mainly the United States. In 1996, Japan's combined central and local government deficit approached 7 percent of the GDP, one of the largest among OECD countries.[17]

Last but not least, due to the continuing regulation of certain domestic sectors, Japan has been suffering from an accumulation crisis, the lack of opportunities to re-invest profits accumulated in the export sector: According to Hirsh and Henry,

The message of the multinationals is this: The low productivity and growth of this over-regulated marketplace no longer work for us. Japanese firms across the board have seen a dramatic deterioration in the break-even points and efficiency of their Japan-based operations.[18]

Reflecting this trend, the former chairman of Toyota Motor Corporation, Shoichiro Toyoda, calls for a "shift from an economy burdened by regulations to one in which the private sector can operate unfettered."[19] The

Exhibit 3.4
Employment and GDP by Sector in 1995

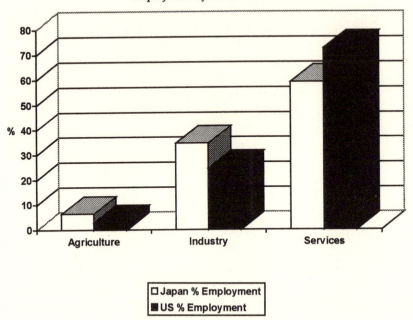

Employment by Sector in 1995

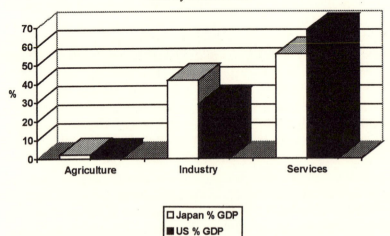

GDP by Sector in 1995

Source: OECD Observer (June/July 1996).

lack of opportunities reinforces the hollowing out of the economy (discussed earlier), eventually feeding into the speculative frenzy that will be discussed in the next chapter.

In short, Japan's early efforts to open her markets to foreign products and competition, especially the hyperliquidity that followed the Plaza Accord, had a mixed impact on her economy. On the one side, it accelerated the country's economic growth, boosting equity and real estate prices. On the other side, it raised the country's already high cost of living, further opening the gap between the country's production and consumption potential, leading to a hollowing out. In the meantime, unfavorable demographics raised the country's government deficit, while deregulation limited investment opportunities in a number of domestic sectors. Life became even more expensive for Japanese consumers, and competition became even tougher for Japanese producers.

To address these new challenges, Japan reversed some of her earlier measures and accelerated others. To contain hyperliquidity and rising asset values, the BOJ tightened up the money supply, raising the official discount rate five times, from 2.5 percent in 1989 to 6 percent in 1990; it also imposed restrictions on land transactions and bank loans. Japan's broad money supply dropped from 10 percent in November 1990 to below 1 percent in 1992 before bouncing back to around 3 percent in 1994 (see Exhibit 3.5).

In the meantime, as part of the ongoing GATT negotiations and the establishment of the WTO, Japan continued to slash tariff and non-tariff trade barriers in line with her major trade counterparts. Specifically, with the exception of some agricultural products and alcoholic beverages, Japan slashed tariffs to 2.6 percent, well below the 3 percent level for the United States and the 2.9 percent level for the European Union.[20] Tariffs continued to drop even further after the establishment of the WTO (see Exhibit 3.6). Product standards and certification systems were adjusted in line with those of other industrialized countries. The Electrical Appliances and Material Control Law, for instance, simplified certification for foreign appliances and electric products. The Measurement Law simplified the procedure for the importation of measurement devices, and a 24-hour import clearance service was established.

Japan further continued to make progress in such highly protected sectors as agriculture and finance. In the agricultural sector, for instance, under pressure from the country's two main beef suppliers, Australia and the United States, Japan reached an agreement that provided a two-stage liberalization of beef imports. In the first stage, from 1988 to 1990,

Exhibit 3.5

Japan's Broad Money Supply Growth

(%)

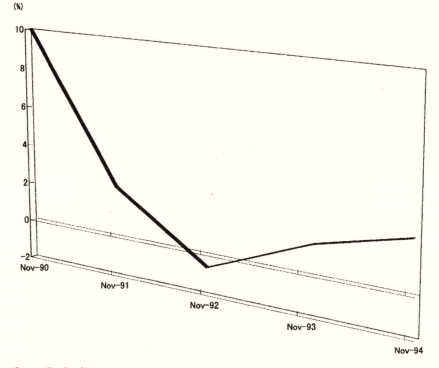

Source: Bank of Japan.

import quotas were raised from 274,000 metric tons to 394,000 metric tons, maintaining a 25 percent tariff. In the second stage, from 1991 to 1993, quotas were raised from 472,000 metric tons to 680,832 metric tons, and tariffs were raised to 50 percent.

In the financial sector, Japan continued to deregulate deposits, securities commissions, and currency transactions.

- June 1992: Revision of laws regulating financial system is approved.

- June 1993: Interest rates on time deposits are fully liberalized.

- October 1994: Interest rates on demand deposits are liberalized.

- November 1996: Deregulation of fixed commissions on securities begins.

- June 1997: The Financial Supervisory Agency (*Kinyu Kantokucho*) is established to oversee the fairness and transparency of the financial system, a function previously performed by the MOF.

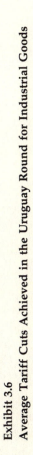

Exhibit 3.6
Average Tariff Cuts Achieved in the Uruguay Round for Industrial Goods

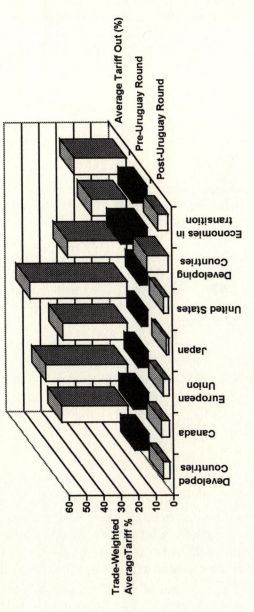

Source: World Trade Organization, 1996.

Exhibit 3.7
Real GDP Annual Growth in Major Industrial Countries for Selected Periods

Country	1983–1987	1994	1995
Japan	4.0	–0.4	1.3
United States	4.0	4.1	3.2
OECD	3.4	3.7	2.7

Sources: The Europa World Year Book 1992/94 (London: Europa Publications); OECD, *Economic Outlook 1994* (Paris: OECD, 1994); International Monetary Fund, *World Economic Outlook* (Washington, DC: IMF).

• 1998: Amendments are made to the Bank of Japan Law to eliminate one of the two former policy-making agencies (the Directors Meeting) and to strengthen the other (the Policy Board), turning it over to the sole policy-making body of the BOJ.

• April 1998: The Big Bang; Foreign Exchange and Foreign Trade Law takes effect, liberalizing cross-border transactions; commissions on stock transactions in excess of 50 million yen are deregulated; investment trusts are created; financial disclosure rules are strengthened; and the diversity and efficiency of financial markets are improved.

The reversal of monetary policy, the continuation of government deregulation, unfavorable demographics, the soaring yen, and tighter land financing rules took a new toll on the economy, again most notably on the banking sector. Tight monetary and fiscal policies, for instance, caused a prolonged economic stagnation, eliminating a risk cushion, a condition for abacus banking. Indeed, Japan's economy slid into the worst stagnation and recession in the postwar period. The GDP dropped from 6.1 percent in 1988 to 5 percent in 1991 and to negative territory by 1994 (see Exhibit 3.7), and with the economy sliding into the recession, unemployment increased from 2.5 percent in 1991 to 3 percent in 1994.

As economic growth declined, real disposable income growth and savings followed suit. Real disposable income growth fell from 6 percent in 1998 to less than .5 percent in 1993, while the savings rate dropped from 16 percent in 1987 to 12 percent by 1994.[21] Low savings in turn lowered the flow of deposits, especially since regulation provided investment alternatives. M2 (a broad measure of money supply) growth declined from about 10 percent in 1987 to 2 percent by 1993, while M2 + CD (certificates of deposit) declined from nearly 12 percent in 1987 to nearly 0 percent in 1993. Such a decline in the flow of deposits in turn compelled banks to raise lending rates and scale back credit. Credit growth rates fell from 5.5 percent in 1990 to nearly 3 percent in 1995.[22]

Economic stagnation and excess capacity turned asset inflation into deflation, eliminating yet another condition of abacus banking. Stock and land prices began to come back to earth, profits dropped, and bankruptcies soared. By 1994, the Nikkei average was back to around 15,000, and land prices dropped by 30 percent, an issue which will be further addressed in the next chapter.

Economic stagnation was associated with diminishing corporate profitability that reduced corporate investment, eliminating a third condition of abacus banking. The profit-to-sales ratio, for instance, fell from 4 percent in 1988 to 1.5 percent in 1993.[23] Lower profitability in turn took its toll on corporate investment and corporate borrowing. Nominal corporate investment growth fell from 18 percent in 1988 to −12 percent in 1993.[24] The annual growth of loans to the property industry fell from 15 percent in 1989 to below 5 percent in 1992. Corporate bankruptcies increased from around 6,000 in 1989 to 12,000 in 1992. In addition, the curtailing of a long-standing BOJ policy of overlending further constrained the ability of banks to extend corporate loans. In fact, in 1990, the BOJ ordered banks to scale back corporate lending by 30 percent.[25]

The loosening up of *keiretsu* relations undermined the loan diversification function of the main bank, eliminating a fourth condition of abacus banking. In 1990, the share of the big six *keiretsu* groups in current income dropped to 13.3 percent, and their share in the workforce dropped to 4 percent from the corresponding shares of 16.9 percent and 4.0 percent in 1985. In the meantime, the percentage of non-financial shares held by banks dropped from around 17 percent in 1988 to around 15 percent in 1997, while the percentage of bank shares held by non-financial firms dropped from 45 percent in 1988 to 40 percent in 1997.[26] The percentage of equity of Bank of Tokyo of Mitsubishi held by other companies dropped from 26 percent in 1990 to 14 percent in 1998.[27]

In short, the tightening of fiscal and monetary policy in the early 1990s eliminated most of the conditions of abacus banking. But what presented the final blow to abacus banking was the disbanding of the *Gosou-sendan Houshiki*, the "escorted convoy" system of financial regulation, the sailing away of the MOF "destroyers" that protected Japanese banks both from within and without competition (see Exhibit 3.8). Specifically, the continued liberalization of demand and time deposits further intensified the

Exhibit 3.8
The Disbanding of *Gosou-sendan Houshiki*

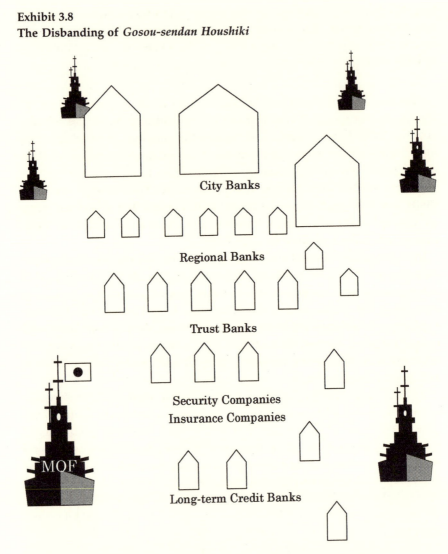

City Banks

Regional Banks

Trust Banks

Security Companies

Insurance Companies

Long-term Credit Banks

competition between the banking and non-banking industries, raising deposit rates. Worse, coming later than earlier, deregulation took full effect at a bad time for the Japanese banking industry, during a period when economic slowdown and asset deflation had already had a pervasive impact. According to Nukazawa,

In the financial sector the regulation and protection of segregated financial industries in the name of preserving the stability of the financial system lasted too long. No doubt it is difficult to get the timing right when outdated regulations need to be removed. The Japanese version of Big Bang now being readied will deal this sector a severe blow just when it is on its knees, and I can sympathize with the people working in it.[28]

Compounding the problem of poor timing of deregulation is the inconsistency in which it was introduced. Specifically, while on the one side the MOF lifted a number of financial regulations, it maintained its tight controls over bank management. Deregulation unleashed competition, but deprived bank managers the freedom to take the appropriate measures to deal with the new environment. As Tanaka observes: "The 1980s saw the rapid deregulation of interest rates, but it did not bring an atmosphere of freedom for banking executives to develop their institutions' operations as they thought best."[29]

In short, under external and internal pressures, Japanese policy makers initiated a number of measures that took the Japanese economy on a roller-coaster ride, known as the bubble economy, and its burst, a course that led to the decline and fall of abacus banking. Competition between banking and non-banking institutions intensified, the interest rate spread turned negative, corporations shifted from bank to equity financing, *keiretsu* relations weakened, economic growth and savings slowed down, and asset values declined.

By the early 1990s, Japanese banks found themselves competing against their U.S. and European counterparts in a fast-paced global economy with more opportunities and more risks. Japanese banks found themselves without the MOF apparatus that made things work, which brought an end to abacus banking and began the banking crisis, issues that will be addressed in the next chapter.

NOTES

1. Quoted in Horvat (1998).
2. Ibid.
3. According to some estimates of the Institute for International Economics in Washington, non-tariff barriers double the cost to Japanese consumers of many imported products. In 1989, for instance, trade barriers cost Japanese consumers 10–15 trillion yen, which translates to between 2.6 percent and 3.8 percent.
4. C. Prestowitz, "Getting Japan to Say Yes," *The Washington Post Weekly*, January 31–February 6, 1994.
5. OECD (1993), p. 49.

6. T. R. Reid, "Lifestyles of the Rich and Foolish," *The Washington Post Weekly*, November 18–24, 1991.

7. R. E. Cole, "Work and Leisure in Japan," *California Management Review* (Spring 1992).

8. Kunio (1979).

9. Lawrence (1998), p. 50.

10. JETRO (1994), p. 9.

11. Japan's population is graying; the percentage of elderly persons is reaching the alarming threshold of 10 percent, and by the year 2000, it will exceed 15 percent, creating a number of problems for the Japanese economy.

12. According to the estimates by the Japanese Ministry of Labor, the labor force was expected to expand by 0.8 percent annually in the first half of the 1990s and by 0.4 percent in the latter part, compared to 1.2 percent in the 1980s, and wages were expected to climb by 30 percent, three times the rate of inflation. See A. Ono, "Making the Most from Japan's Untapped Labor Resources," *Economic Eye*, Vol. 13, No. 1 (Spring 1992).

13. Economic Planning Agency (1995).

14. Ibid.

15. A. Pollack, "Japan's Companies Moving Production Overseas," *New York Times*, August 29, 1993.

16. "Shellshocked by the Yen, Japanese Companies Still Find Ways to Cope" (1995).

17. OECD (1996), p. 3.

18. M. Hirsh and E. K. Henry, "The Unraveling of Japan Inc.," *Foreign Affairs*, Vol. 76, No. 2 (March–April 1997), p. 11.

19. S. Toyoda, "Dismantle Japan, Inc.," *New York Times*, April 17, 1997.

20. Japanese Ministry of Finance.

21. OECD (1995, 1996).

22. OECD (1997), p. 19

23. OECD (1994b), p. 23.

24. Ibid.

25. Ibid., p. 106.

26. "Stock Sales Cut into Cross-Holdings," *Nikkei Weekly* (editorial), January 11, 1997, p. 11.

27. B. Bremner, E. Thornton, and I. Kunii, "Fall of a Keiretsu: How Giant Mitsubishi Group Lost Its Way," *Business Week*, March 15, 1999.

28. Nukazawa (1998), p. 27.

29. Tanaka (1998), p. 22.

Chapter 4

The Banking Crisis

Imagine, after walking in on the middle of a poker game, that you are asked to choose which player will be the ultimate winner. Would you automatically pick the player with the biggest pile of chips?

If your answer is no, then you believe in risk adjustment. You realize that it matters how a player won its chips. If he did so with one lucky bet, he is unlikely to be the overall winner.

—Mark Hulbert[1]

The market goes to extremes—both on the downside and upside—but has a nasty habit of eventually steering itself back towards rationality.

—Robert Sobel[2]

For over a century, Japan's banks financed the country's successful industrialization. In the 1950s and the 1960s, they financed the country's transformation from a labor-intensive economy to a capital-intensive economy. In the late 1970s and the early 1980s, they financed the country's transformation from capital-intensive industries to technology-intensive industries and the overseas expansion of the country's large corporations. In the late 1980s, they rescued American counterparts, climbing to the summit of the world's financial system, drawing both the fear and the admiration of the Western world. In 1986, seven of the world's ten largest corporations were Japanese, compared to none 30 years earlier (see Exhibit 4.1).

Japan's banks reached the summit of the world economy without any special effort, any active or subtle strategy, collecting and counting "chips," equities, and real estate with the abacus, the ancient Chinese calculator, and within the "escorted convoy" system. Yet as was the case in the ancient Greek myth of Sisyphus, who rolled his rock all the way to the top of a hill, only to have it roll down again, Japanese banks could not hold onto their position at the top. Their abacus calculators could not account for a major change in the banking environment, the liberalization and deregulation of the world markets, which turned banking from a simple accounting procedure to a complex, risk-management procedure. Their abacus calculators could not detect and prevent the speculative mania that swept the country—it rode along with it. Like the Sisyphus rock, banks rolled downhill, dragging along the entire economy and its notorious gatekeepers, the omniscient regulators of the MOF. By 1998, one out of ten of the world's largest banks was Japanese, compared to seven out of ten in 1988 (see Exhibit 4.1).

In addition, Japanese banks lost clout even in the Asian region. In 1998, for instance, Japan's banks failed to register in the top ten lenders in the region, and many of the country's largest banks and financial corporations suffered heavy losses, drawing lower debt grades by credit institutions. Tokai Bank, for instance, dropped three grade notches, Sakura Bank dropped four, and Daiwa dropped five (see Exhibit 4.2). Nikko Securities' bond rating dropped one grade notch, Nomura Securities dropped three and Yamaichi dropped five, eventually filing for bankruptcy (see Exhibit 4.3). According to some estimates, Japan's banks and savings and loan associations have accumulated close to $400 billion, even $500 billion of non-performing assets, a figure that dwarfs that of the U.S. banking crisis in the 1980s.[3]

In this sense, Japan's speculative mania and the banking crisis that followed can find parallels to a number of manias that swept Europe and the United States in the previous centuries:

• The speculation and collapse of the South Sea Company and the government debt in the early eighteenth century in England and the panic of 1720; the Canal mania in the late eighteenth century and the panic of 1793; the speculation in the railways, wheat, and equities in the nineteenth century and the panics of 1847 and 1890, which led to the near collapse of the Baring Bank.[4]

• The Mississippi company speculation and the panic of May 1720 in France; the

Exhibit 4.1
The World's Ten Largest Banks (1982–1998)

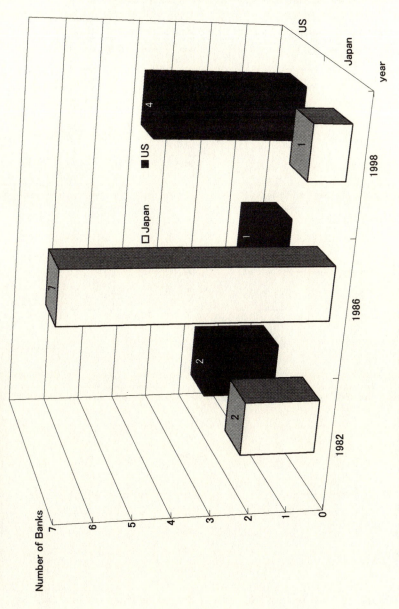

Source: Statistics Bureau, Japan Statistical Association (various years).

Exhibit 4.2
Standard & Poor's Long-Term Issue Credit Ratings (1991–1998)

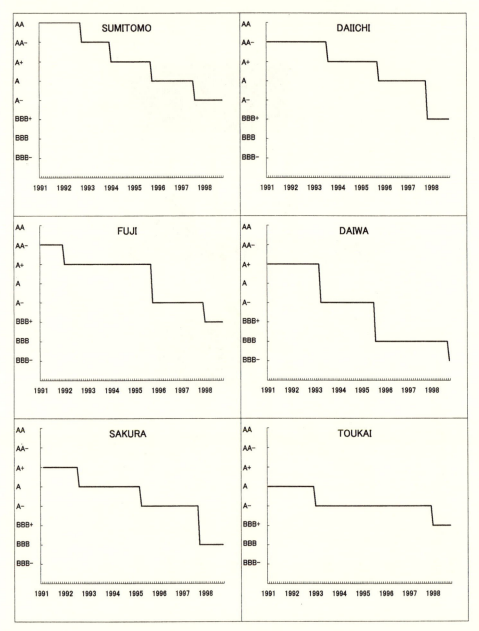

Source: Compiled from various Standard & Poor's publications.

Exhibit 4.3
Standard & Poor's Bond Ratings (1986–1997)

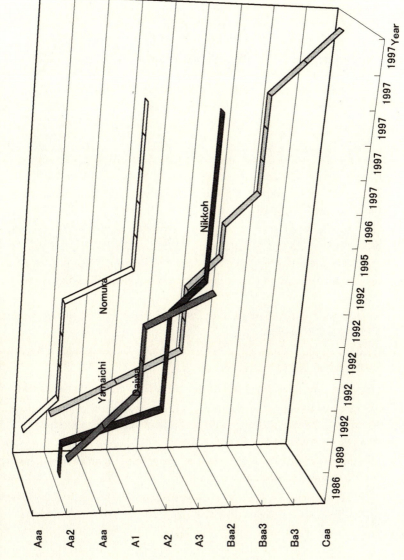

Canals and the Paris bank speculation and the panic of 1827; the regional bank crisis and panic of 1837; the speculation in the stock of new banks and the panic of 1882; the overlending to the industrial sector that led to the panic of 1907, which spread to Italy; the currency speculation, which led to the panic of 1958; the speculation in commodities and the panic of 1799 in Germany; the speculation in heavy industries, in Credit Mobilier, and in new German banks, which led to the Hamburg panic of 1844; the speculation in new banks, broker banks, and construction banks, which led to the panic of 1873.

• The speculation in the Wildcat banks of the free banking era in the United States and the crush of 1837; the speculation in the railroads, public land, and gold, which led to the panic of 1857; the speculation in trust companies and the crush of 1907; the speculation in stocks, real estate investment trusts, and the Eurodollar market, which led to the crush of 1974–1975.

As has been the case with previous speculative manias, Japan's speculative mania and the banking crisis that followed can be traced to a mob psychology driven by the complacency and euphoria of Japanese investors and bankers and their failure to apply the basic principles of risk management in evaluating investment alternatives, as well as the failure of regulators to take preemptive measures to curtail the mania and avert the crisis. Specifically, Japan's speculative mania and the banking crisis were caused by a combination of the following factors:

• The hyperliquidity created after the 1985 Plaza Accord, which provided the funds for speculation.

• Deregulation of the banking industry, which intensified competition and provided the incentive for speculation.

• The introduction of *jusen*, which provided the vehicle of speculation.

• The lack of investment opportunities in the real sector of the economy, which prompted the nation's large corporations to shift their investments from productive to speculative activities.

• The failure of investors and banks to apply the principles of risk management in evaluating investment alternatives.

• The failure of the MOF and the BOJ to diagnose the bubble and take preemptive action to burst it earlier rather than later.

Arguing these contentions in more detail, the remainder of this chapter extends the discussion of the previous chapter to explain how the Japanese economy reached from the Plaza Accord of the mid-1980s to the banking crisis of the mid-1990s. Specifically, the chapter demonstrates how the burst of the economic bubble in the late 1980s and the early 1990s eliminated the conditions of abacus banking, leaving banks in a risky world without the freedom, incentive, and expertise to handle it.

As discussed in the previous chapters, in the first four decades that followed the end of World War II Japanese banks enjoyed a cozy, risk-free environment. In such an environment bank management was a routine game, an abacus exercise rather than a risk management problem. Exchange rate controls limited foreign currency risks. An active industrial policy that identified industries to be protected by domestic and foreign competition (and rescued, if necessary) limited systemic or aggregate risk. A BOJ policy of overlending virtually eliminated liquidity risk. Long-term and *keiretsu* relations between banks and their clients and rising asset values virtually eliminated individual risk. An "escorted convoy"-style MOF banking regulation system protected banks from foreign and domestic competition, further limiting systemic credit risk. Steady economic growth allowed banks to move in tandem and to compete on high-volume, low-profit-margin lending, taking a steady share of an ever-larger pie.

After the 1985 Plaza Accord, the cozy, low-risk environment was replaced by a rather uncertain, risky one. In such an environment, bank management was much more than a routine game, an abacus exercise—it was a risk management game. The sharp yen appreciation increased currency risks. A passive industrial policy no longer identified industries to be protected from foreign and domestic competition, raising systemic credit risks. The abandonment of the policy of overlending by the BOJ raised liquidity risk. The disbanding of the "escorted convoy"-style banking regulation system no longer protected banks from internal and external competition, further raising systemic credit risk. The weakening of long-term and *keiretsu* relations between banks and their clients and declining asset values, especially land values, raised individual risks. The slowdown in economic growth no longer allowed banks to move in tandem and to engage in *bogai* (the "detour" or cover-up of short-term losses).

Against all Okurasho efforts to hold it at bay, risk had arrived in the banking system. It had always been present, but high-speed economic growth for half a century had outpaced and overpowered it. This experience had created a sense of complacency in the banks and in their regulatory masters. The implicit government guarantee of all banks had made them cocky, and this sentiment, mixed with the excitement of the bubble economy, created a dangerously intoxicating cocktail of lending recklessness.[5]

Though gradual, the shift from a low-risk environment to a high-risk environment engaged banks in a speculative mania, a roller-coaster ride, all the way to the summit and then all the way down to the bottom of the world banking system. Specifically, the yen appreciation, financial liberalization, and the monetary easing that followed the Plaza Accord had a contradictory impact on Japanese banks. On the one side, money easing increased liquidity, stimulated economic growth, and raised asset prices, creating complacency about economic fundamentals and traditional banking risks. On the other side, financial deregulation intensified competition between banks and money market mutual funds, raising deposit interest rates and turning the interest rate spread negative, especially during the bubble years. In addition, rising corporate profits and a stronger yen allowed large corporations to raise funds internally or in the Eurobond and equity markets. Many of the country's largest corporations would issue equity or debt, not to finance their investment needs but to add excess capacity or to deposit it in banks, taking advantage of the high interest rates.

In short, the yen appreciation, financial deregulation, and hyperliquidity provided the funds, and deregulation provided the opportunity and incentive for engaging banks in speculative activities. Finding themselves with excess liquidity, a negative interest rate spread, and a declining demand for low-risk corporate loans, banks had to search for new clients in the high-risk, small- and medium-sized corporations and in real estate and any other investment opportunities opened up by deregulation. Hyperliquidity and government deregulation led banks to restructure both the asset and liability sides of their balance sheet, increasing their exposure to traditional and non-traditional banking risks. On the liability side, a larger proportion of their deposits was exposed to interest rate risks. On the asset side, a larger portion of their loan portfolio was subject to individual and systemic credit risk. Specifically, banks redirected loan portfolios from large corporate clients to small corporate clients, from the traditional manufacturing sector protected by government regulation to the service sector, especially to the real estate that is at the whim of market forces. Indeed, reflecting this shift, investment in services and in real estate in particular accelerated during the bubble years. Between 1985 and 1991, investment in services and finance doubled, while investments in real estate tripled (see Exhibit 4.4).

Accommodating the shift in bank lending was a newly introduced institution, the *jusen*, which borrowed money from trust banks, long-term banks, and agricultural credit institutions and then lent it to individual

Exhibit 4.4

Loans Outstanding by Industry (1975–1995)

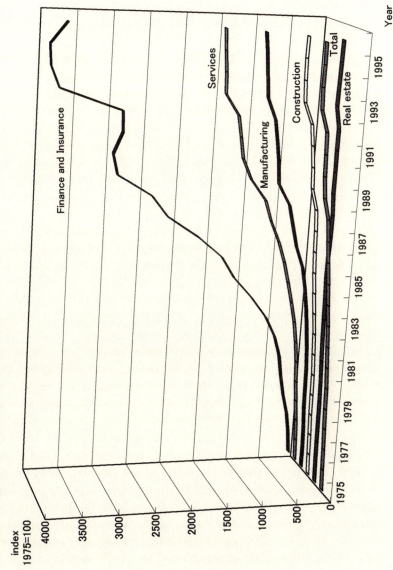

Source: Statistics Bureau, Japan Statistical Association (various years).

mortgagees.[6] In this sense, *jusen* was supposed to serve the government's efforts to elevate the standard of living of the Japanese people in the late 1980s by assisting them in buying their own apartments. It did not take long, however, before *jusen* turned into speculative vehicles that allowed banks and other credit institutions to channel funds to scores of land speculators, including the *Gene-con* (general contractors or land developers).

Gene-con borrowed huge amounts of money for the development of residential and commercial real estate. But as many of the regulations regarding land use still remained in place, limiting the land supply, *Gene-con*'s rush to acquire land raised land prices sharply, making it more profitable to purchase land just for the purpose of selling it for a quick profit. Land development turned into *tochi-korogashi* (speculative land churning), which drove prices even higher, attracting even more players and creating a real estate bubble.

Eventually, speculation spread from *jusen* to the country's large manufacturing corporations in the export sector. With the strong yen hurting exports and with investment opportunities in the domestically oriented sector limited, the country's corporations reached for opportunities in the financial sector through what is known as *zeitek*, or money technology (that is, speculative investments).

Traditionally, Japanese corporations shunned active management of their cash assets and disdained investment profits as less honorable than profits earned from basic industrial operations. But when Washington began forcing up the yen, many Japanese companies had little choice but to turn to *zeitek* techniques to make up for profit squeeze they faced on the operating side. Early in 1987 fully 50 percent of the profits of Tokyo Stock Exchange–listed companies were derived from investments rather than operations.[7]

As deposit interest rates began to rise, corporations turned to another form of *zeitek*, the issuing of corporate equity or debt, not to finance the expansion of their business but to deposit the proceeds into banks, a practice that added liquidity to the banking system. Indeed, during the bubble years, capital market fund-raising by the stock exchange–listed corporations increased from 49 percent to 58.4 percent of the total fund-raising in the domestic market.[8] Over the same period, deposits rose faster than the GDP, outpacing loan growth (see Exhibit 4.5). Between 1985 and 1990, the bank liquidity ratio (ratio of cash, deposits, and short-term securities to monthly sales) increased from 1.2 to about 2.2.[9] In

Exhibit 4.5
Bank Deposits, Loans, and GDP (1960–1994)

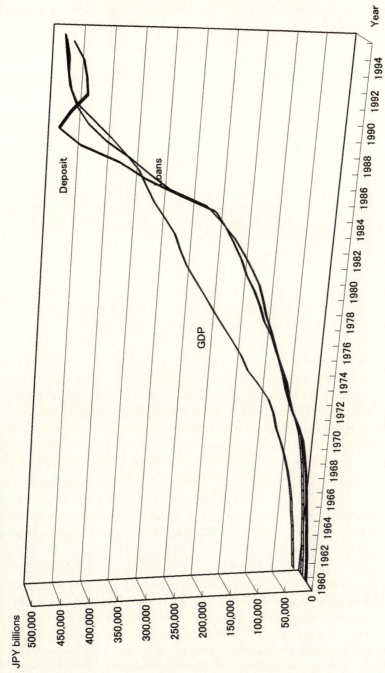

Source: Statistics Bureau, Japan Statistical Association (various years).

practice, this meant that banks were eventually faced with an "embarrassment of the riches": a higher stream of deposits and a lower stream of loans.

The banks were in a dilemma. Their best customers—big corporations—were not only walking away from them to raise money on the stock market, they were also paying back early borrowings. The big firms would then turn around and, loaded with cash from their stock market dealings, put large amounts of it into bank accounts. The banks very soon discovered that they were facing an embarrassment of the riches on the deposit side of the ledger but a shortage of borrowers to loan the money to on the other.[10]

In addition, as more and more internal or equity financing replaced bank financing, a new institution, "core banks," replaced the institution of "main bank." As Shikano puts it,

Banks are losing their competitive advantage against client firms, which have been supported by the restrictive policy of the Government toward the capital market, and are required to cope with these challenges. Large firms in Japan are now trying to designate the top three to five banks as their "core banks" among banks instead of a single main bank.[11]

The replacement of the institution of the main bank with the institution of the core banks has two important implications for the banking industry. First, banks have become less effective in performing their traditional function as "main banks," as brokers in loan syndicates and the risk diversification associated with it. The decline of the role of the main bank further means that main banks have become less effective in monitoring the corporate performance of their clients. Second, as banks turned from corporate lenders to corporate borrowers, they could no longer perform their conventional function of imposing fiscal discipline and control over corporate boards; neither could impose a system of accountability to stockholders, as is the case in Western market economies. Such a system simply did not exist.

An important source of discipline—the prudential oversight traditionally exercised by banks over their firms—was lost. Many companies were quite carried away and raised funds not because they needed them but simply because the money was so cheap. It was common bubble-economy practice for big corporations to raise large sums from the stock market at a cost of less than half a percent and then simply put the money into bank deposits where they earned 6 percent.[12]

One of the problems with this period is that nobody asked the stockholders what they thought, and nobody cared. During these years banks lost their traditional oversight function because firms no longer needed them. Yet the system of accountability to stockholders that operates in the United States and other markets had not been developed.[13]

With little accountability to their stockholders, freed from the bank discipline, and with easy money raised in the equity and debt markets, *zeitek* turned into a reckless expansion of productive capacity, especially in the early 1990s, when operation rates declined substantially (see Exhibit 4.6). *Zeitek* further engaged corporations into an acquisition spree in the West, especially in the United States. Many of the most precious U.S. assets—record labels and movie studios, theme parks, technology companies, and hotel and ski resorts—including CBS Records, Columbia Pictures, MCA, and Rockefeller Center—came under Japanese ownership.

The interest of Japanese corporations in American assets was not just confined to corporate acquisitions; it extended to portfolio and real estate investments, U.S. corporate stocks, government securities, and real estate. As of 1989, Japanese had invested the cumulative total of about $300 billion in the U.S. economy. According to estimates reported in *Tokyo Business Today*, Japanese companies purchased $13 billion worth of equity in 1990. Throughout the 1980s, the Japanese financed about one-third of the U.S. government deficit. By 1989, Japanese investments in real estate had reached $14.8 billion.

It did not take long before the speculative mania that swept the land and real estate markets spread over to the equity markets and to every object of speculation. Rising asset values fed into this frenzy, a mob psychology where investors rushed to buy assets not because of their fundamental values but because of the potential of quick appreciation, or by imitating others who had become rich that way. According to Kindleberger,

Mob psychology or hysteria is well established as an occasional deviation from rational behavior. We have its elements in many economic models: the demonstration effect, which leads developing countries to adopt consumption standards beyond their capacity to produce for themselves; keeping up with Joneses in consumption; refusing, when income declines, to cut consumption systematically with the increase in consumption that occurred when income rose (the Duesenberry effect).[14]

Exhibit 4.6
Production Capacity and Operating Rate (1981–1996)

Index (1990=100)

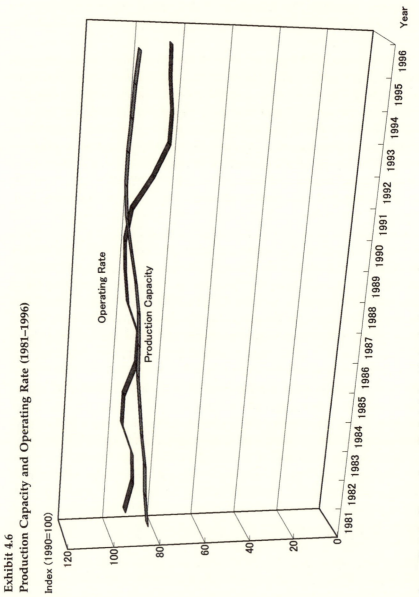

Source: Statistics Bureau, Japan Statistical Association (various years).

In short, excess liquidity and deregulation provided both the funds and the incentive, while *jusen* provided the vehicle that allowed Japanese executives, real estate brokers, investment bankers, and *yakuza* (organized crime members) to engage in a speculative mania comparable to the Dutch tulip mania of the seventeenth century and the South Sea mania of the eighteenth century, mentioned earlier in this chapter. And as was the case with previous manias, investors and the bankers who financed them ignored almost every principle of risk management. First, they ignored the direct relationship between risk and interest rate premium (i.e., the riskier the investment, the higher the interest rate premium). Ignoring this principle, Japanese investors valued assets not in relation to economic fundamentals, such as the prospective returns and appreciation potential of an asset, but in relation to other already overvalued assets. Foreign and domestic equities, real estate, and even fine art were compared to already overvalued Tokyo real estate prices. How else could one explain and justify the astronomical prices Japanese investors paid for fine art and foreign real estate? In 1989, for instance, Tomonori Tsurumaki, the Japanese real estate broker, paid $51.7 million for Picasso's "Les Noces de Pierrette" and $400 million for a resort in Southern Japan. In 1990, Ryoei Saito, the owner of a large manufacturing firm, paid $82.5 million for van Gogh's "Portrait of Dr. Gachet" and another $78.1 million for Renoir's "Le Moulin de la Galette." In 1989, the Sazale Group paid $110 million—a record of $1.2 million per room—for the Bel-Air Hotel.[15] Real estate companies, *jusen*, housing-loan corporations, and credit cooperatives lent *yakuza* billions of dollars in the 1980s.[16] Japanese collectors paid a record $40 million for Vincent van Gogh's "Sunflowers." Mitsui Real Estate overpaid $235 billion for the Exxon building,[17] and Mitsubishi Real Estate paid $850 million for New York's Rockefeller Center.

Second, taken by a herd mentality, Japanese investors and the banks that financed them ignored another principle of risk management, diversification (the spread of an investment portfolio over several projects and regions). Japanese banks and other credit institutions, for instance, limited their lending to a few individuals and institutions. Tokyo-Kyowa, for instance, lent $376 million (or 40 percent of the institution's total outstanding loans) to a Mr. Takahashi, an entrepreneur with cozy ties with MOF officials. Credit co-ops did even worse than that; close to 40 percent of them extended large loans to single clients, illegally![18] Japanese banks further concentrated their financing activities in a few geographic areas, such as California and Hawaii. "Rather than fanning

Exhibit 4.7
Purchase versus Sale Value of Selected Japanese Investments

Asset	Acquirer	Purchase Value $billions)	Sale Value ($billions)
MCA	Matsushita	6.1	5.7
Pebble Beach	Minoru Isutani	.84	.30
Arco Plaza	Minoru Investments	.62	.30
Western Maui	Abe International	.29	.15
Hyatt/Regency Waikoloa	HRW Ltd.	.32	.10

across the United States, Japanese commercial banks have clustered their operations in California, where five are now among the ten biggest, and 20 percent of all bank assets are now Japanese owned."[19] Japan's investment in real estate is particularly evident in Hawaii, where the Japanese have invested $1.9 billion, a figure that represents close to 70 percent of foreign investment in the island.[20] As confirmation of this herd mentality and concentration, Japanese banks commanded the same investment grading. "The propensity of the Japanese to act in objective concert can be seen all over the map. Following roughly similar policies, Japanese commercial banks have ended up with roughly similar international credit ratings, and many of them are tops—AAA."[21]

Unfortunately for Japanese investors and their financiers, the nation's banks, and *jusen,* easy money did not last forever. Neither did robust economic growth and rising asset prices. As the art market declined along with real estate prices, Japanese banks found themselves with repossessed paintings and with real estate properties that could fetch only a fraction of the amount the banks had lent to their previous owners (see Exhibit 4.7). By 1995, many Japanese companies were divesting part or all of their early acquisitions, including Matsushita Corporation, which sold 80 percent of its holdings in MCA for $5.7 billion, taking a huge loss in yen terms, and Rockefeller Center, which had gone bankrupt.[22] To make matters worse, the yen appreciation and the collapse of the Tokyo real estate market undermined banks' domestic and international equity holdings. In fact, every time the Nikkei stock average drops, it has a significant negative effect on banks' balance sheets. A decline in the Nikkei from 19,563 to 15,000 cuts Asahi Bank's profit from $1,052 to $430 and the Bank of Tokyo's from $599 to $110 (see Exhibit 4.8). In fact,

Exhibit 4.8
Banks' Latent Profits

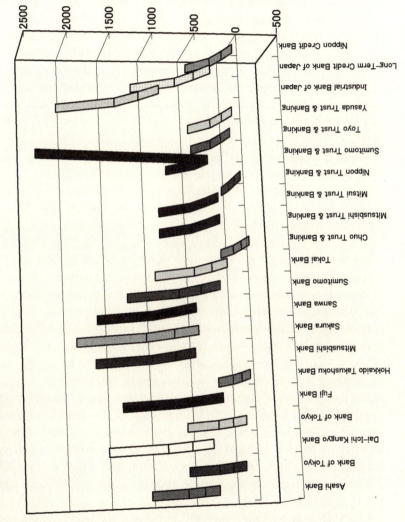

Source: Adapted from Nomura Research Institute.

as banks strove to survive on interest income, they accelerated their reckless lending, accumulating additional non-performing assets.[23] Even as recently as 1996, at least half of the 21 major Japanese banks reported losses due to write-offs of bad loans, with the remaining following suit shortly thereafter.[24]

In short, Japan's banking crisis can be attributed to a combination of factors—the hyperliquidity that provided the fuel, the deregulation that provided the incentive, and the introduction of *jusen* that provided the vehicles for turning hyperliquidity into non-performing assets. But is this not similar to the U.S. savings and loans crisis of the 1980s? In a sense, it is. In both countries, the banking crisis can be attributed to a combination of high-risk investment ventures, overoptimism, and poor risk management. According to White,

The bulk of the insolvent thrifts' problems, however, did not stem from such fraudulent or criminal activities. These thrifts largely failed because of an amalgam of deliberately high-risk strategies, poor business judgements, foolish strategies, excessive optimism, and sloppy and careless underwriting, compounded by deteriorating real estate markets.[25]

Yet the banking crisis in the two countries differs in four ways. First, U.S. thrifts have been more experienced in handling financial crises. Specifically, U.S. thrifts had faced similar conditions in the late 1960s during the Vietnam War, when rising inflation pushed deposit interest rates higher, hurting bank profitability. Second, having made early strides in deregulation, U.S. banks were more diversified in terms of products and services supplied than Japanese banks. In 1994, for instance, loans accounted for around 58 percent of total assets, compared to 65 percent in Japan (see Exhibits 4.9 and 4.10). Third, in the United States, regulation rarely restricted bank managers' freedom to make decisions. Fourth, in contrast to Japanese banks, U.S. banks were much smaller, which made them more flexible in dealing with the rapid changes in their market environment brought about by deregulation. But why did the MOF and the BOJ fail to diagnose the bubble and take measures to burst it earlier, rather than later?

The MOF failed to diagnose the bubble and the banking crisis because it was part of the problem rather than part of the solution. In fact, as early as 1992, the MOF knew that some *jusen* were already in trouble, but the cozy ties with the institutions they were supposed to oversee prevented them from taking prompt and diligent action. "*Jusen* docu-

Exhibit 4.9
Bank Net Loans in Japan (1960–1996) (percent of total assets)

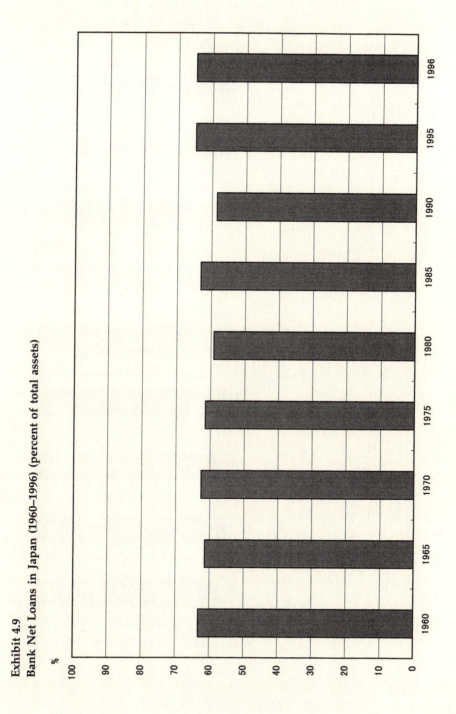

Exhibit 4.10
Bank Net Loans in the United States (1980–1995) (percent of total assets)

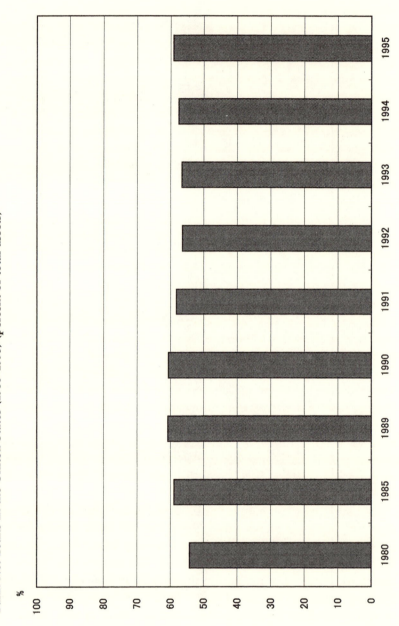

ments released recently show that the ministry's Banking Bureau has been dysfunctional. The ministry knew that the *jusen* were on the brink of bankruptcy back in 1992, but decided to take no action."[26] In some cases, such as that of Daiwa's subsidiary in the United States, Japanese regulators asked Japanese officials to *bogai*, or conceal losses from the U.S. regulators because MOF officials placed their own interests ahead of the general public that they were supposed to protect; but there was a good reason for that—*amakundori*, or "descent from heaven."

Upon retirement, *amakundori* allows former bureaucrats with the MOF to be employed by the institutions they used to regulate. But even before they get there, even when they discharge their normal duties as regulators, they frequently socialize with bank executives, accepting generous gifts. According to Williams,

As Japan's banks were lending promiscuously to real-estate speculators, golf-course builders and gangsters in the late 1980s and early 1990s, an elite group of former bureaucrats was in a position to act. At that time, some of today's ailing lenders had Finance Ministry and Bank of Japan alumni in crucial jobs as auditors, directors, executives, and presidents.[27]

But why did the BOJ fail to diagnose the economic bubble and take preemptive measures to burst it? The BOJ failed to diagnose the bubble because of its belief of a "New Era" for the Japanese economy, a supply side–driven expansion without the threat of inflation, as suggested by the traditional Phillips inflation-unemployment trade-off. Specifically, though Japan's economy unemployment rate fell to levels below what is considered a "natural rate," the BOJ did not expect a relapse of inflation, and for good reason (see Exhibit 4.11). Due to the rising yen, falling import prices, and rising productivity, a decline in the unemployment rate did not translate into higher but into lower inflation (see Exhibits 4.12 and 4.13).

In short, during the bubble years, having found themselves with excess liquidity, Japanese banks either directly or indirectly through the *jusen* extended credit to *Gene-con* and other investors based on inflated bubble values rather than on economic fundamentals. So when the bubble burst, banks were left with non-performing assets. In this sense, the Japanese banking crisis was the result of the failure of the Japanese system as a whole rather than the failure of individual banks, as was the case with the savings and loans crisis in the United States in the 1980s. Nurtured in an environment of fast economic growth, *keiretsu* relations, and tight

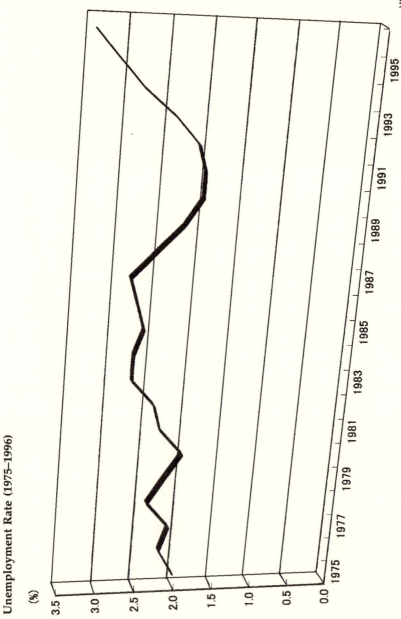

Exhibit 4.11
Unemployment Rate (1975–1996)

Source: Statistics Bureau, Japan Statistical Association (various years).

Exhibit 4.12
Japan's Domestic Wholesale Price Index (1981–1996)

index
(1990 = 100)

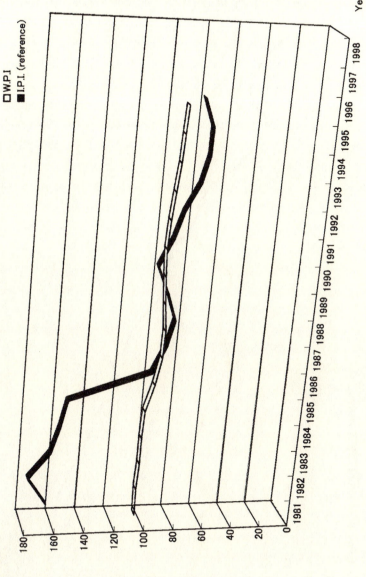

Source: Statistics Bureau, Japan Statistical Association (various years).

Exhibit 4.13
Japan's Labor Productivity (1960–1996)

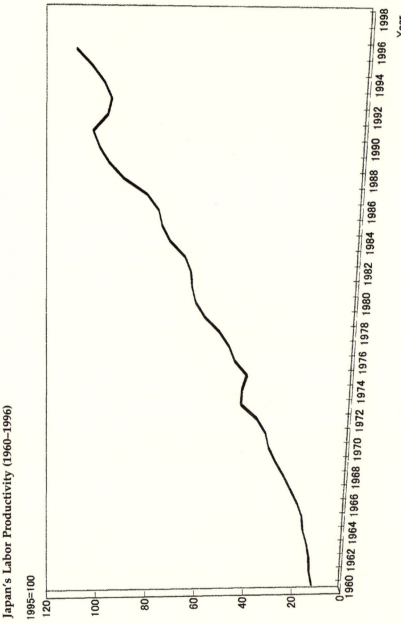

Source: Statistics Bureau, Japan Statistical Association (various years).

government regulation, Japanese bankers lacked the ability, the incentives, and the skills to manage funds in a risky environment.

A cause and a symptom of the economic stagnation, the banking crisis has crippled the ability of the monetary authorities to stimulate the economy out of the stagnation, but it has seriously damaged their reputation. With many MOF and BOJ officials involved in bank scandals, the Japanese public's trust and faith in bureaucracy has been seriously shaken, paving the way for a new government structure that shifts power away from appointed bureaucrats to elected politicians. And that is also true for Chinese banks, an issue that will be further addressed in the second part of this book.

NOTES

1. M. Hulbert, "There Is a Price to Pay for Ignoring Risk," *New York Times*, December 6, 1998, p. 6.

2. R. Sobel, "Going to Extremes," *Barron's*, January 2, 1999.

3. Estimating the size of the banking crisis is rather difficult due to poor disclosure requirements.

4. For a detailed discussion of manias and panics, see Kindleberger (1989).

5. Hartcher (1998), pp. 155–156.

6. In fact, agricultural credit institutions contributed 45 percent of *jusen* funds. For details, see OECD (1995), p. 51.

7. Burstein (1988), p. 44.

8. For details, see OECD, *Economic Outlook* (Paris: OECD, 1990/1991), p. 89.

9. OECD, *1991 Annual Survey* (Paris: OECD, 1991), p. 98.

10. Hartcher (1998), p. 74.

11. Shikano (1998), p. 93.

12. Hartcher (1998), p. 71.

13. Ibid., p. 73.

14. Kindleberger (1989).

15. Powell and Takayama (1992).

16. "How the Mob Burned the Banks" (1996).

17. Hartcher (1998), p. 71.

18. Ibid., p. 135.

19. Burstein (1988), p. 216.

20. J. Larson, "Japanese Invasion Welcomed in Hawaii," *American Demographics*, Vol. 13, No. 12 (December 1991).

21. Burstein (1988), p. 216.

22. Mitchell (1997), p. 5.

23. Ibid.

24. Sapsford (1996b).
25. White (1991), p. 117.
26. "Loan Crisis Makes Clear" (1996b).
27. Williams (1996), p. 1.

Part II

The Rise and Fall of Abacus Banking and the Looming Banking Crisis in China

Chapter 5

The Rise of
Abacus Banking in China

How far back in history must one dig to trace the roots of banking in China? Some historians dig all the way back to the Song dynasty period (960–1274), when China had developed an elegant central banking system. Others start with the Ming dynasty period (1368–1643), when the country had created a commercial economy based on money and credit. And a third group begins with the Quing dynasty, especially the period 1845–1895, the establishment of European and Japanese colonialization.[1]

Irrespective of how far back in history one reaches, China's banking has always been a tightly controlled industry with little competition and the risks associated with it, especially in the last two centuries. In the nineteenth century, for instance, banking was tightly controlled by the government and by the guilds, which restricted entry into the industry, fixed loan rates, and rationed credit to their members. In the first three decades that followed the communist victory, China's banking industry turned into a state-owned industry within a central plan that determined the flow of funds into and out of the industry. In this sense, banking was a routine administrative procedure rather than an active credit risk management operation. Bank lending was primarily extended to the corporate sector, and lending interest rates were set according to the form of ownership and communist party *guanxi* relations, reflecting political priorities rather than risk premiums. This means that banks were not true banks in the capitalist sense; they were not for-profit enterprises, but government departments with fiscal responsibilities, such as monitoring the money traffic between the government coffers and the corporate sector. Almost all deposits were administratively collected as "profits" of SOEs and rationed to various industries according to government priorities.[2] The same applies to non-banking institutions such as credit cooperatives, normally run by provincial and local governments. Bank and credit co-op managers lacked the freedom, the expertise, and the incentives to allocate credit according to the principles of risk management.

In the two decades that followed the 1978 reforms, especially during the high-growth period (1978–1993), a number of state-owned banks were allowed to diversify their operations outside the central plan; a Western-style independent central bank was introduced; efforts were made to separate banking from other business activities and to limit the influence and control of state and local governments over bank financing; and new institutions, known as non-bank financial enterprises, were allowed to operate side by side with state banks and credit cooperatives.

In spite of these reforms, banks continued to be run as government departments, monitoring the money traffic in and out of the state treasury, rather than as true for-profit banks. A large portion of their deposits continued to come from budgetary allocations, SOE "profit" deposits, or "voluntary" salary reductions, and their managers continued to be appointed by government bureaucrats and communist leaders, allocating credit according to central planning priorities. In this sense, bank managers played the role of abacus bankers, recording the money flows, rather than true bankers, allocating credit according to the principles of risk management. In addition, as a government monopoly carrying out the sovereign power to issue money, banks enjoyed seigniorage income. This was especially the case during the high-growth era, when rising savings and deposits allowed banks to expand seigniorage, financing the deficits of both the central government and the SOEs.

Arguing this hypothesis in more detail, this chapter briefly reviews China's attempts to develop her economy and modernize her banking industry, especially during the high-growth era (1978–1993), and investigates how such attempts laid the foundation of the Chinese abacus banking system. Specifically, this chapter reviews China's failed attempts to develop her economy and banking industry in the thirteenth and nineteenth centuries, as well as in the first three decades of the communist rule, and compares and contrasts it with the 1978–1993 high-growth period.

As the conventional economic wisdom emphasizes, the welfare of a country does not depend on the quantity and the quality of its resources alone, but on the social regime, the environment that shapes the ownership relations and the allocation of these resources. Countries with poor economic resources have often prospered because of the right social regime, ownership relations, coordination mechanisms, the absence of strong vested interests, and government regulation. Conversely, countries with rich economic resources have been made poor due to wrong ownership relations, poor coordination and management, government policies, and the presence of strong vested interests, which has been the case in China.

A country rich in economic resources, especially human resources, China has missed several opportunities to develop herself and prosper because social inertia and government regulation have constrained the efficient allocation of her resources and the diffusion of new technology. According to Arayama and Mourdoukoutas,

China has missed several opportunities to turn inventions into innovations because of a number of economic, political, social and cultural barriers. Powerful guilds and government regulations limited competition and the diffusion of new technology throughout the economy. An open and fluid social structure lured rising merchants away from industry to landholdings and government bureaucracy. A fair heredity system gave younger sons less incentive to assume entrepreneurial ventures.[3]

To be specific, China has already missed three opportunities to develop herself. China's first opportunity to develop dates centuries back, well before Europe, the United States, and Japan pursued their own development at the end of the Song dynasty, when the country's economy was more advanced than the rest of the world.[4] But China did not capitalize on this advantage. It did not reach to grasp and colonize the world, as Europeans later did, because her institutions constrained the creation of a world market frontier for her products and the diffusion of new technology.

China's second missed opportunity dates back to the middle of the nineteenth century, when the country unsuccessfully defended herself against the Europeans, the Russians, and the Japanese, who sought a world market frontier of their own. In fact, China's defeat by all three powers resulted in the division of the country into spheres of foreign influence. In addition, at this crucial time, China was caught in a fifteen-year bloody civil war known as the Taiping Rebellion, which further divided the country and stalled economic progress. But even after the end of the Taiping Rebellion, government regulations, xenophobic protests such as the Boxer Rebellion of 1900, low labor mobility, and powerful professional guilds in particular slowed the country's indus-trialization.

China's third missed opportunity dates back to the 1950s and the 1960s and deserves little comment. At a time when China's neighbors were rushing to join GATT, Chinese leaders were pulling out of it to debate the way to socialism rather than the way to world markets.[5] Within this debate, opening up China to the rest of the world was perceived as a danger rather than an opportunity for economic development, and the same applies to private ownership and markets that were replaced by state ownership and central planning. In fact, during the peak years of the Cultural Revolution (1966–1969), China's foreign trade dropped by 13 percent in nominal terms, while exports accounted for less than 3 percent of GDP.[6]

The country's economic resources were placed within a Soviet-style central planning system of nationalized enterprises, farm collectives, pro-duction targets, and tight commodity and resource price controls. Spe-cifically, economic resources were assigned to SOEs and collective enterprises (CEs) and were allocated according to the priorities set by a central plan. The SOEs and CEs were managed by managers recruited from the ranks of both party members and local government officials. This in turn meant that corporate managers lacked the freedom, the in-centive, and the expertise to adjust inputs and outputs to changing mar-ket conditions and to develop new products and processes, a source of sustainable competitive advantages.

China's failure to take advantage of her early opportunities to develop herself is not confined to the real sector of the economy but extends to her banking industry too. During the Song dynasty, for instance, the country had developed a state-of-the-art central monetary system, well before England and other European nations developed their own. Yet China failed to create a modern banking system because of the presence of powerful guilds that limited competition and maintained the status quo. "Bankers' guilds were common although not universal. Where they existed, the credit of nonmembers suffered. Nonmember banks had to offer higher rates of interest and undertake business that members would not consider."[7] In this sense, Chinese guilds were different, more protective, than European guilds. According to King,

The guilds cannot be compared directly with their European counterpart since each played [a] different role in a different form of society. But the Chinese guilds tended to control the various trades with the intention of maintaining the *status quo*, by setting conditions of apprenticeship, new entry, credit terms, and techniques of production.[8]

China has also made progress in banking in the second part of the nineteenth century, but the Taiping Rebellion and again powerful guilds restricted the development of the economy and the banking industry. The Taiping Rebellion, for instance, disrupted trade and led to merchant loan defaults. Guilds once again limited banking to their members, creating in essence an oligopoly. "Cooperating in crises, stabilizing the methods of banking businesses, facilitating trade by provision of credit, and furnishing a link between the market systems of China—all these were recognized functions of native banks and their associations."[9]

Under the earlier days of communist rule, the banking industry was reconstructed in the form of a single bank, the People's Bank of China (PBC), a government-owned bank that had branches throughout the entire country. Specifically, the PBC was established on December 1, 1949 as a state conglomerate of three communist banks, and it was placed under the control of the Government Administration Council. The PBC soon set up municipal and provincial branches, field branches, offices, suboffices, and supplementary saving units throughout the country and placed them under the supervision of the Financial Department of the Military Control Commissions of the local governments.[10] The PBC further controlled credit cooperatives, normally set in remote rural areas where the bank could not set its own offices. The PBC further instated credit limits and quotas that in effect rationed credit according to the priorities set by the central planners.

By the mid-1950s, the PBC was placed under the direct control of the State Council, which replaced the Government Administration Council, and eventually under the Ministry of Finance. According to Lu and Yu,

Under the central planning, the PBC was essentially an accounting subsidiary of the Ministry of Finance. There were no specialized roles for the central bank and commercial banks in the system. The PBC functioned simply as a monobank to provide assistance for the fulfillment of the state physical production plan.[11]

In the meantime, the PBC forced out of business or took over private banks and integrated independent credit cooperatives. In this capacity, the PBC was not just a bank but the entire banking industry.

In Communist China, the People's Bank in fact served as the entire banking system; her monetary function was therefore comprehensive. It channeled saving towards investment, and supplied loans for working capital; it also had to control the total supply of money so as to avoid inflationary or deflationary pressures, especially the former.[12]

An entire industry rather than an individual bank, the PBC was a state monopoly with the ability to control credit and the money supply. In this sense,

Unlike the Western commercial banks, the People's Bank was monopolistic; it was expected to keep nearly all enterprise funds as deposits. These features, plus the fact that there was no legal reserve requirement, gave the Bank an infinite ability to expand credit as long as such credit was not used for wages or agricultural payments.[13]

In practice, this means that the PBC had a monopoly over money creation and the seigniorage income associated with it, which often became a source of conflict between Beijing and provincial governments. "Since bank loans are 'free' or nearly free goods in disguise, local authorities would employ all kinds of administrative measures to restrict the outflow of bank funds and zealously seek more of these cheap credits."[14]

As a state credit monopoly, the PBC did not have to be concerned with traditional and non-traditional banking risks. The lack of foreign and domestic competition and state ownership posed little or no risk to its major clients, SOEs, and their ability to repay their loans. Centrally determined wages and prices made input and output demands steady and predictable. This lack of concern for risk is evidenced in the interest rate structure, which reflected political priorities rather than risk premiums. Corporate interest rates, for instance, were determined not according to the creditworthiness of individual corporations but according to the ratio of government to private ownership—the larger this ratio, the lower the interest rate. "The outstanding feature of the structure was that the interest rate moved inversely with the degree of socialization of the credit recipients, state enterprises being subject to the lowest rate and private enterprises to the highest."[15] In 1955, for instance, private enterprises could borrow from the PBC at 1.35 percent, while SOEs could borrow at .48 percent.[16]

As a state credit monopoly, the PBC performed another "microfinancial" function, that of central accountant and auditor of the corporations—recipients of the credit. According to Hsiao,

The microfinancial, or supervisory, function refers to economic surveillance over individual enterprises via careful scrutiny of the financial conditions of each unit. In this respect, the Bank is to act as a central accounting and auditing agency that can check the performances of the firms thereby spurring them to greater efficiency and adherence to plans.[17]

Therefore, the PBC played a similar role of the "main bank" in Japan, which also monitored the performance of the corporations—*keiretsu* members—with three major differences. First, the "main bank" was still a private bank rather than a state-owned one, and therefore it promoted the interests of the *keiretsu* members rather than the interests of the "people." This meant that its stockholders and not the government bureaucrats could hire and fire the bank board and management. Second, as a private bank, the main bank was subject to reserve requirement regulations that limited its ability to create credit. Third, the "main bank" and its corporate customers operated under a market environment rather than a centrally planned one.

In short, due to social inertia, China missed several opportunities to develop her economy and modernize her banking system, especially in the first three decades of communist rule when banks were government departments, instruments of central planning and not true banking institutions. But what about China's fourth effort to develop herself? What did it change for banks?

China's fourth and ongoing bid to join the world markets and develop herself dates back to the late 1970s and coincides with the resumption of globalization (i.e., the increasing integration and interdependence of world markets). Joining Japan and the Asian newly industrializing economies (NIEs), the country pursued an aggressive export-led industrialization strategy supported and reinforced by a number of reforms that loosened the grip of central planners on the economy. In the manufacturing sector, for instance, initial reforms allowed a limited number of enterprises to market their products outside the central plan directives, make personnel decisions, retain and reinvest profits, and set their own bonus and welfare payments system. Subsequent reforms expanded this program to the entire SOE sector and changed the tax law to give SOEs a number of write-offs and depreciation allowances, switching the financing of SOEs from outright grants to loans and connecting corporate financing to creditworthiness. More recently, reforms gave SOEs the power to control wages, make production decisions, recruit middle-level managers, and retain and distribute part of any realized profits. The government further introduced a dual-price mechanism that allowed the coexistence of both government-set prices and market-determined prices for the output of SOEs. SOEs that exceeded their production quotas could sell their excess output in the market, where prices exceeded those set by the government.

In contrast to previous attempts to join the world economy, China's ongoing attempt to develop herself got off on a good start, at least during the 1978–1993 high-growth period. Foreign investment rose sharply from a few billion dollars in the early 1980s to over $100 billion in 1992 (see Exhibit 5.1). Exports soared from a few billion dollars in the 1970s to $180 billion by 1995 (see Exhibit 5.2). Chinese products have been flooding Western markets, and the country runs surpluses with major trade partners, especially the United States. Foreign investment and exports have in turn propelled the country's robust economic growth bounds, especially in the late 1980s and the early 1990s (see Exhibit 5.3).

China's success in reforming her economy has extended to her financial and banking industries, where reforms included the establishment of an independent, American-style central bank, commercial banks, state policy banks, and non-bank financial institutions (see Exhibit 5.4). In pursuing this objective, China's central bank, the People's Bank, reduced the number of its branches from 30 (one for each province) to twelve (one for each newly established district), making it difficult for provincial governments to influence its decisions. Further financial and banking reforms included the expansion of securities markets, the introduction of foreign market swaps, and non-bank financial institutions.

- In 1979, the Bank of China was separated from the People's Bank of China and began to play a more active role in raising funds and allocating credit to various projects.
- In 1980, the Interim Rules on Promoting Economic Coalition allowed banks to operate their own business.

Exhibit 5.1
Foreign Direct Investment in China (1983–1997)

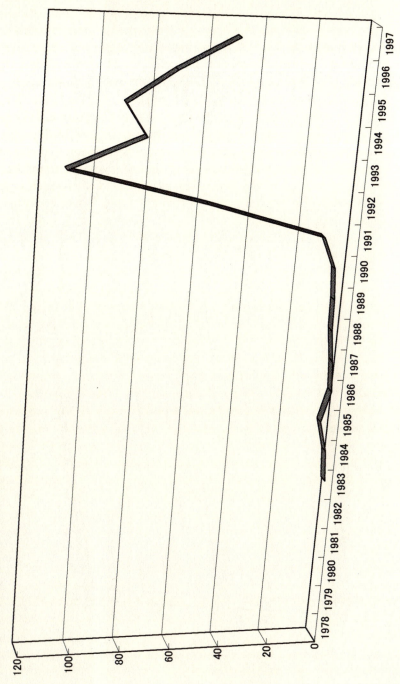

Source: State Statistical Bureau (various years).

Exhibit 5.2
Foreign Trade in China (1950–1995)

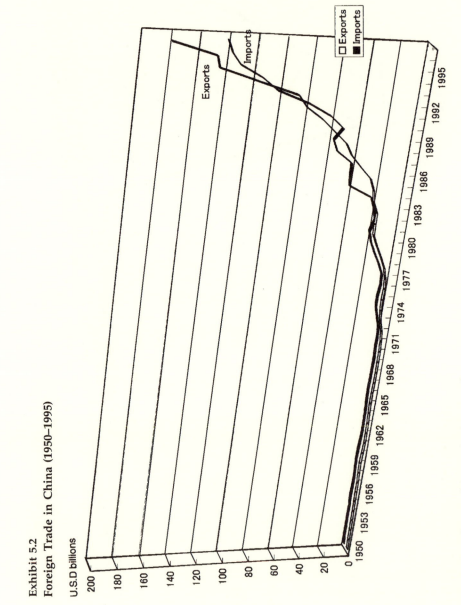

Source: State Statistical Bureau (various years).

Exhibit 5.3
Real GDP Growth in China (1952–1996)

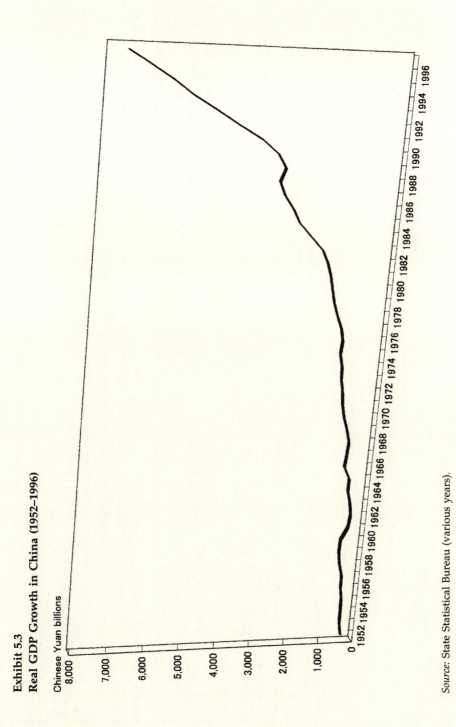

Source: State Statistical Bureau (various years).

Exhibit 5.4
Financial Organization in China

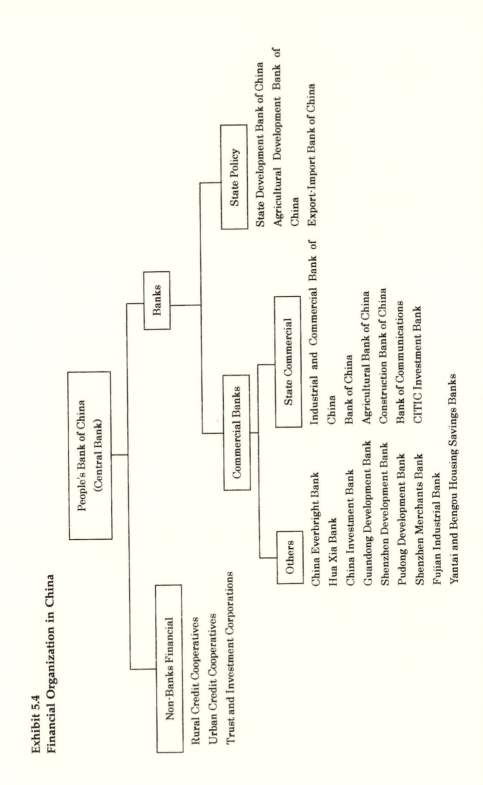

- In 1981, Beijing expanded the government and corporate securities markets. The Beijing government further allowed local governments to introduce non-bank institutions, such as the International Trust and Investment Corporations (ITICs) that raised funds for less reputable companies that had no access to domestic equity markets or foreign bank financing.

- In 1984, the Peoples' Bank became in effect China's central bank.

- In 1986, the government introduced foreign exchange swap centers, setting the stage for the creation of a foreign exchange market.

- In 1988, banks were allowed to set deposit interest rates to float within a specified range over the official rates. The government allowed the operation of secondary bond and equity markets.

- In 1994, Beijing allowed open market operations in the bond and foreign exchange markets.

- In 1995, Beijing passed the Commercial Bank Law and the PBC Law, which separated banking from non-banking business, further limiting the influence of provincial and local governments on PBC policies.

- In 1996, on a trial basis, Beijing allowed a nationwide interbank market.

As was the case in Japan, China's early success to develop herself reinforced a number of conditions of abacus banking. Robust economic growth, for instance, fueled personal income and savings growth. Indeed, according to statistics published by the Bank of China, between 1982 and 1993 personal per capita income increased sixfold, from around 400 yuan to over 2,400 yuan. Over the same period, per capita savings increased fifteenfold, from 100 yuan to 1,500 yuan. According to IMF estimates, published in the 1996 World Development Report, for the 1978–1994 period China's savings averaged 36 percent of the GDP, compared to 35 percent of the GDP for Japan for the 1961–1973 period, and 33 percent over the 1983–1994 period, reaching close to RMB2.3 trillion (see Exhibit 5.5). High savings in turn boosted bank deposits, which increased almost fortyfold for the period 1980–1997, compared to 2.5 times for the United States (see Exhibits 5.6. and 5.7). Driven by exports and foreign investment, which in some provinces like Guangdong reached 124.57 percent and 24.91 percent of the GDP in 1994, respectively, the country's growth further increased foreign exchange reserves from around $20 billion in 1992 to around $135 billion in 1997.

Along with interest rate controls, monetary expansion in turn has allowed the Chinese state banking industry "to earn large amounts of *voluntary seigniorage,* simply by printing money to satisfy growing

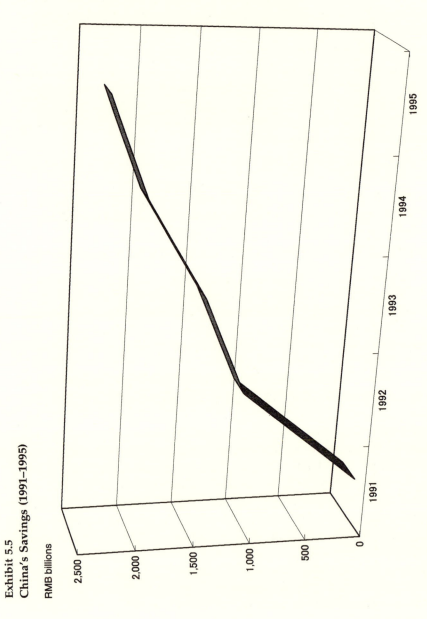

Exhibit 5.5
China's Savings (1991–1995)

RMB billions

2,500

2,000

1,500

1,000

500

0

1991   1992   1993   1994   1995

Source: State Statistical Bureau (various years).

Exhibit 5.6
Bank Loans in China (1980–1997) (percent of total assets)

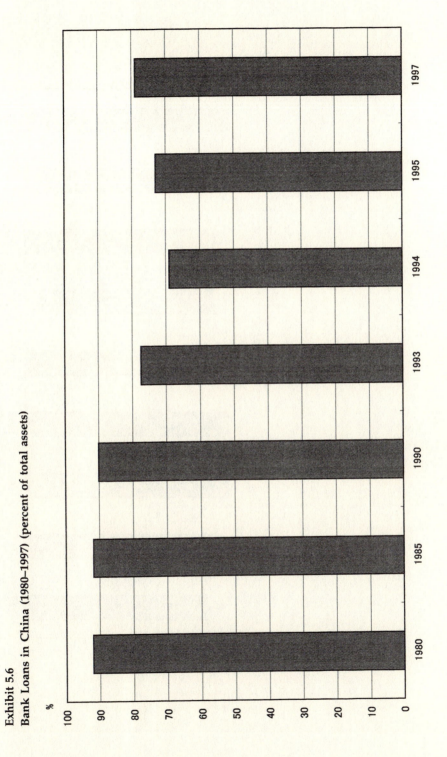

Exhibit 5.7
Bank Loans in the United States (1980–1995) (percent of total assets)

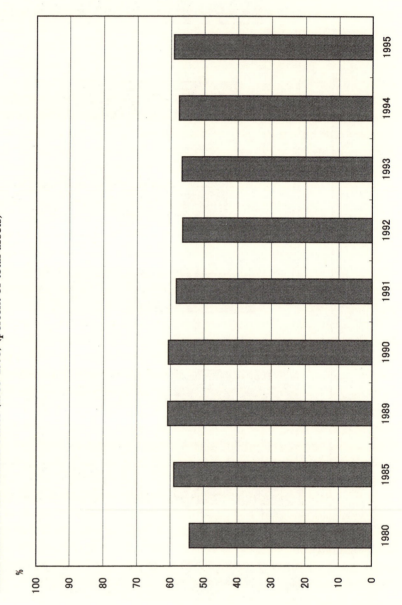

demand."[18] At the same time, rising deposits have allowed the Chinese government to finance SOE debt, keeping them afloat without printing new money or raising taxes. "Without the very high savings ratio the government would have either had to let these loss making 'enterprises' sink or subsidize them through the printing press."[19] Indeed, loans to SOEs have risen sharply. Bank loans soared from a few hundred billion RMB in the early 1980s to over 2,000 billion RMB by the late 1980s (see Exhibit 5.8).

Loans to SOEs have turned monetary growth into an endogenous rather than an exogenous variable, set within political and technical parameters rather than by the PBC. As Yu and Xie conclude in a study of money aggregation and control in China, "At present, supply of monetary base is rather endogenous. Political, institutional, and technical barricades prevent the PBC from satisfactory control of monetary base."[20]

But have these reforms advanced far enough? Are China's economy and the banking system in particular catching up with the rest of the world? In a sense, compared to her arrogant centralized communist system of the past, especially that of the Cultural Revolution, the answer to these questions is yes. China has made a great leap forward toward the liberalization, decentralization, and modernization of her economy and banking system.

In another sense, compared to the rest of the world, the answer is no. China's economy and banking system has yet to match its Western counterparts in efficiency and effectiveness. Specifically, since 1978, a period of resumption of globalization, the rest of the world has not stood still waiting for China to catch up. Even market economies like the United States have been pursuing policies to further limit the presence of government in the economy by deregulating industries that have traditionally been under government protection; and both European and Latin American economies have been deregulating and privatizing their industries.

In the finance sector in particular, the United States and Europe have forged ahead with interest rate liberalization, the introduction of new products, and the elimination of barriers that limited interindustry and interregional competition. Banks have been further shifting their focus away from traditional financial intermediation business to fee-based business, such as asset management on behalf of their clients.

That is not the case for China, however, which has yet to equal the rest of the world in modernizing her economy and banking industry. In spite of the extensive reforms and impressive performance since 1978,

Exhibit 5.8
Bank Assets (1980–1997)

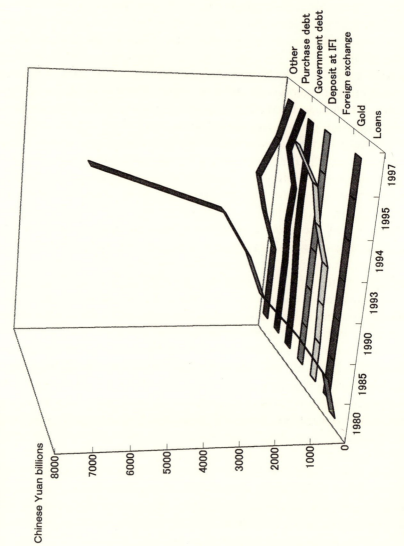

Chinese Yuan billions

Source: State Statistical Bureau (various years).

the Chinese government by and large remains the majority owner of SOEs and the successors of CEs, township and village enterprises (TVEs). This means that their board and management are either directly or indirectly controlled by the Communist Party or national, provincial, and town governments, which appoint the managers who run them.

Appointed by a Communist Party–selected board, managers' primary objective is to maximize "people's" welfare, that is, the welfare of the Communist party, the national, state, and local government bureaucrats, the large number of SOEs, and the surrounding community. Even the emerging private enterprises and joint ventures are at the mercy of provincial and local governments, as they must enjoy good relations with them if they want to be and remain in business.

The same arguments can be made regarding the banking sector, where bank assets are almost 100 percent owned by the government, compared to about 30 percent in Argentina and Mexico.[21] As Mookerjee and Peebles observe: "During the 1980s and continuing into the 1990s the monetary system, together with the state industrial sector which it was created to serve, have remained the least reformed parts of the economy."[22] Wei and Zeckhauser are more emphatic:

For more than a decade, China has been talking about reforming its financial sector, cleaning up its bad loan problems. Some progress has been made, but far from enough; reform is painfully slow. It has not seemed urgent, and it is tied to complex problems of reforming state-owned enterprises.[23]

Indeed, in spite of the many financial liberalization measures announced, the state banking system continued to account for roughly two-thirds of all financial assets, a figure that is probably much higher if many of the bank-owned ITICs are included in the calculations (see Exhibit 5.9). In fact, in 1994, there was only one "privately owned" ITIC, the Shanghai AJ Finance, with RMB 2.4 billion in 1995. In 1997, bank deposits accounted for almost 80 percent of total bank assets in China, compared to 60 percent in the United States (see Exhibits 5.10 and 5.11). And China's central banking continues to display a mix of an independent central bank and a central planing instrument, displayed in the traditional "operational principles of central planning"—that is, unified planning (the central bank rations credit to the banking industry), fund availability (banking liquidity controls), account division (the independence of specialized banks from central banking), and interbank lending.[24]

In practice, this means that credit planning is still in effect in China,

Exhibit 5.9
Financial Assets Distribution (1986–1994)

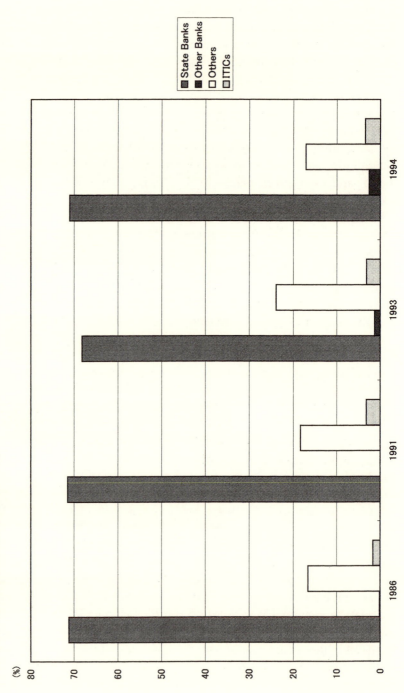

Exhibit 5.10
Bank Deposits in China (1980–1997) (percent of total assets)

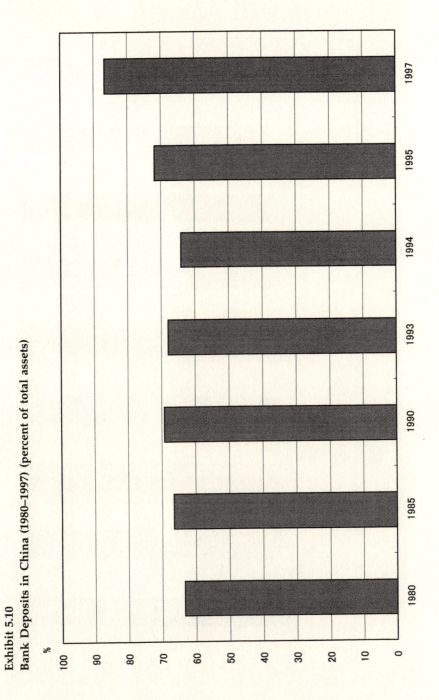

Exhibit 5.11
Bank Deposits in the United States (1980–1995) (percent of total assets)

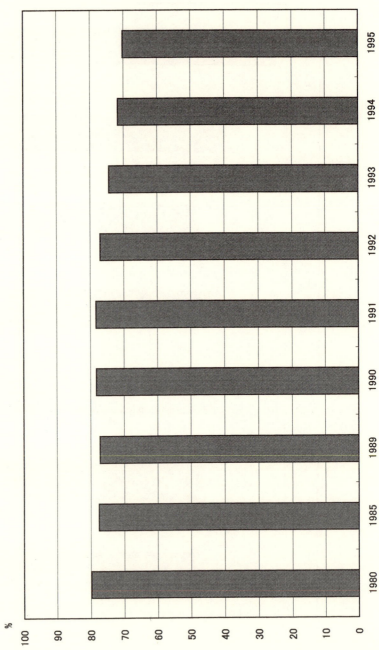

and the PBC pulls the strings to have it implemented. The PBC, for instance, "combines all banks' fund sources and uses, which are aggregated from the banks' regional branches. The national credit plan controls credit uses, both quantitatively and qualitatively, by specifying mandatory annual credit targets."[25] In addition, the PBC injects funds to banks unable to meet loan demand by SOEs and adjusts interest rates to accommodate credit plan targets. The PBC further continues to control interest rates that allow banks to earn seigniorage. This means that Chinese banks have a long way to go before they are transformed into sound financial institutions, as defined by the market. As Melloan observes: "It appears that whatever might be happening to the banking system, it remains a very long way from becoming a financial structure that allocates capital effectively, as banks do in well-run market economies."[26]

Banks by and large remain government departments, operating within a central planning environment and promoting the welfare of the "people" rather than true enterprises operating in a market system and promoting the interests of their stockholders. As Kime puts it,

China's state banking system functions essentially as an agency of the government, "selling" deposits much as a finance ministry would sell government securities. In effect, one agency of the Chinese government borrows from the non-state public and "lends" the money to another part of the government, the state enterprise sector.[27]

Bank managers are recruited from the ranks of Party members and government bureaucrats appointed by Communist Party-controlled boards, and that constrains their freedom to allocate credit according to the principles of risk management. Bank managers, therefore, lack the will and the freedom to assume risks and to adjust their inputs and outputs to changing market conditions. For instance, they have limited freedom to evaluate the performance and to even lay off excess labor or introduce technological processes that may displace labor, as is often the case with the banks of market economies.

Bank managers have little freedom to allocate credit outside of the parameters of the credit plan that continues to be biased toward SOEs, which absorb close to 80 percent of overall credit.[28] Coming from the ranks of government bureaucrats and the Communist Party rather than from business schools, Chinese bank managers lack the skills to understand, analyze, and appraise traditional and non-traditional banking risks. In fact, China has a large shortage of professional managers. After all, this is the country that for centuries looked down on economics and business education, especially during the communist regime, which denounced capitalist management or reduced it to just an engineering operation.[29] Reflecting the attitudes toward business education, the percentage of economic, finance, and management graduates in the total number of university graduates declined from an average of 10.3 in the period 1928–1947 to 2.1 in the period 1966–1976, and it remained at 3.6 in the period 1977–1985.[30]

Given these constraints, the rational choice for the government-appointed managers is to confine themselves to routine and predictable businesses (i.e., expand the volume of lending rather than the quality of lending or venture to the genuine and unpredictable business of developing new products and services). As J. Thomas Macy observed in the 1998 World Forum on Asia, management standards have improved, but China's banks, even its best ones, are still way behind their Western counterparts, particularly in areas such as investment technology. To put it differently, volume lending rather than quality lending or innovation has been the business strategy of Chinese banks, a strategy reflected in the size of China's banks. In 1945, for instance, with more than $30 billion in assets and close to $2.5 billion in profits, China's four state banks— Bank of China, Industrial and Commercial Bank of China, China Construction Bank, and Agricultural Bank of China—occupied the first four out of the top ten positions of Asia's largest banks.[31]

To sum up, the Chinese banking industry has always been a tightly regulated industry, especially during the early communist era, when government ownership and central planning reduced it to a treasurer of the Ministry of Finance. But even during the later communist era, even after the 1978 reforms, banks largely remained under government ownership and control, and bankers continued to act as government accountants, monitoring the money flows between households and government departments, rather than as credit risk managers, with two differences. First, robust economic growth boosted savings and lending to SOEs. Second, it made money flows less predictable than before, especially since corporate clients were exposed to the wild swings of the global economy in the aftermath of the Asian crisis, an issue that will be addressed in the next chapter.

NOTES

1. For a detailed discussion, see King (1965).
2. Determined within the central plan, SOE profit is more an accounting rather than an economic concept.

3. Arayama and Mourdoukoutas (1999), p. 49.

4. One could even trace China's attempt to create a world market frontier even earlier than that, back to the Han dynasty (206 B.C. to 220 A.D.) and the construction of the "Silk Road."

5. In fact, China was a founding member of GATT in 1948 but it dropped out after the communist victory.

6. For a detailed discussion, see Harding (1987), ch. 6.

7. King (1965), p. 97.

8. Ibid., p. 11.

9. Ibid., p. 97.

10. Ibid., p. 20.

11. Lu and Yu (1998), p. 148.

12. Ibid., p. 93.

13. Hsiao (1971), p. 90.

14. Lu and Yu (1998), p. 159

15. Ibid., p. 129.

16. Hsiao (1971), p. 130.

17. Ibid., p. 91.

18. Kime (1998), p. 14.

19. Zhang (1998), p. 1.

20. Yu and Xie (1999), p. 43.

21. "A Survey of Banking in Emerging Markets," *The Economist*, April 12, 1997, p. 12.

22. Mookerjee and Peebles (1998), pp. 152–153.

23. Wei and Zeckhauser (1998), p. 365.

24. Lu and Yu (1998), pp. 150–151.

25. Ibid., p. 151.

26. G. Melloan, "Asia Revives, but Whither Japan and China?" *Wall Street Journal*, March 2, 1999, p. A19.

27. Kime (1998), p. 16.

28. Fry (1999).

29. Indeed, China, a country rich in labor, is poor in specialized labor, especially skilled management.

30. Xu-Yao, Ke-Chun, and Chan-Min (1989).

31. "A Survey of Banking in Emerging Markets," pp. 5–48.

Chapter 6

The Fall of
Abacus Banking in China

A bank lives on credit. Till it is trusted it is nothing; and when it ceases to be trusted it returns to nothing.

—Walter Bagehot[1]

For almost two decades since the late 1970s, globalization, the increasing integration and interdependence of world markets, has shown the world its bright side, especially to the emerging economies of Asia and most notably to China. It has provided them with a genuine opportunity to develop themselves. Fewer trade restrictions, for instance, have made it easier for these economies to sell their labor-intensive products to Western markets. Fewer capital restrictions have allowed foreign investment to pour into their factories. Lower ideological tensions and improved international relations allowed communist countries like China access to Western commodity, technology, and capital markets, which propelled the country's robust economic growth, as discussed in the previous chapter.

By the mid-1990s, globalization began to show the world and the economies of Asia in particular its dark side, that of intensified competition, price destruction, and declining local currencies. In this sense, globalization has turned from a source of opportunity to a source of uncertainty that threatens to slow down or even reverse the early gains that these countries have made in developing their economies. Globalization has further turned into a major challenge to the institutions and policies that for many years have supported the successful entry of these countries into world markets, especially the banking institutions that have been enjoying an almost risk-free environment.

Globalization's dark side is more visible and evident in Asian NIEs and in Japan, coming off a system of highly protected and regulated domestic markets that eliminated competition and the risks and uncertainties associated with them. For instance, in Japan, discussed in Part I of this book, globalization has contributed to the disbanding of the "escorted convoy" system and the intensification of domestic competition that have led to the eventual decline and fall of the abacus banking system and the banking crisis.

Globalization's dark side is less visible and less evident in China, which has been a latecomer to the world economy and therefore under less pressure to open her economy to foreign products and competition. Due to a low degree of integration in world markets, as manifested in the continuing tight currency and interest rate controls, the Chinese economy seems to have weathered the crisis that ravaged the other Asian economies. Her currency remained stable, and the conditions for the abacus banking industry, discussed in the previous chapter, remained intact. This also could explain why China has thus far avoided a full-blown banking crisis.

Yet China has not completely escaped from the Asian crisis. In fact, even before the Asian crisis began, the country's economy suffered from excess capacity, the piling up of inventories, and intensified competition. Export prices have been falling sharply, and foreign capital flows have been stalled or even reversed. In addition, China suffers from two fundamental problems—the lack of an expanding world market frontier for her products and the inability to innovate, that is, to turn new technologies into new products and processes, thus creating sustainable competitive advantages associated with them.

China's lack of an expanding world market frontier and her inability to innovate have taken their toll on her economy and her banking industry in particular, eliminating most of the conditions that supported and reinforced the abacus banking strategy.

- Commodity prices have been declining.
- Government regulation and protectionism have been weakening.

- Economic growth has slowed down.
- The interest rate spread has turned negative.

   Arguing these points, this chapter takes a close look at the Chinese
economy since the mid-1990s, especially since the aftermath of the Asian
crisis, and explains how external and internal pressures have been changing the rules of the game for banks, eliminating most of the conditions
for abacus banking. Specifically, this chapter discusses how a late entry
into the world markets, large size, and social inertia constrain the country's ongoing bid for economic development and narrow the horizons
and choices of China's banking industry, which continue to survive on
seigniorage income.
   As discussed earlier, globalization, especially the easing of ideological
tensions and the improvement of international relations between former
socialist countries and the countries of market economies, has offered
China a genuine opportunity to expand her trade and capital flows to
the rest of the world and to develop herself. Indeed, for almost two
decades since the 1978 reforms, foreign investment, technology transfer,
and robust exports have propelled the country's economy to grow by
leaps and bounds, attracting once again both the fear and the admiration
of China's nearby neighbors and her faraway trade partners.[2]
   Yet, as has been the case in the past, the country's genuine bid to
develop herself has encountered a number of external and internal pressures. External pressures come from China's lack of an expanding world
market frontier for her products as manifested in rising trade tensions
with her trade partners, most notably with her major trade partner, the
United States, which has been experiencing rising trade deficits (see Exhibit 6.1).
   Chinese/U.S. tensions are further manifested in China's difficulty in
complying with WTO requirements for a full WTO membership, stem-
ming from the country's poor timing in joining such an organization.
Specifically, China joins the world market under the WTO regime, which
is a formal international organization that can discipline country members that do not play by the rules, especially members that pursue industrial targeting or other protectionism. Not only does the WTO have
the mandate to discipline members, but its rules cover a broad spectrum
of issues, including property rights and environmental protection, two
areas where China has been repeatedly criticized by the United States
and other WTO members. Besides, today the United States needs Asian

Exhibit 6.1
U.S. Trade Deficit with China (1985–1997)

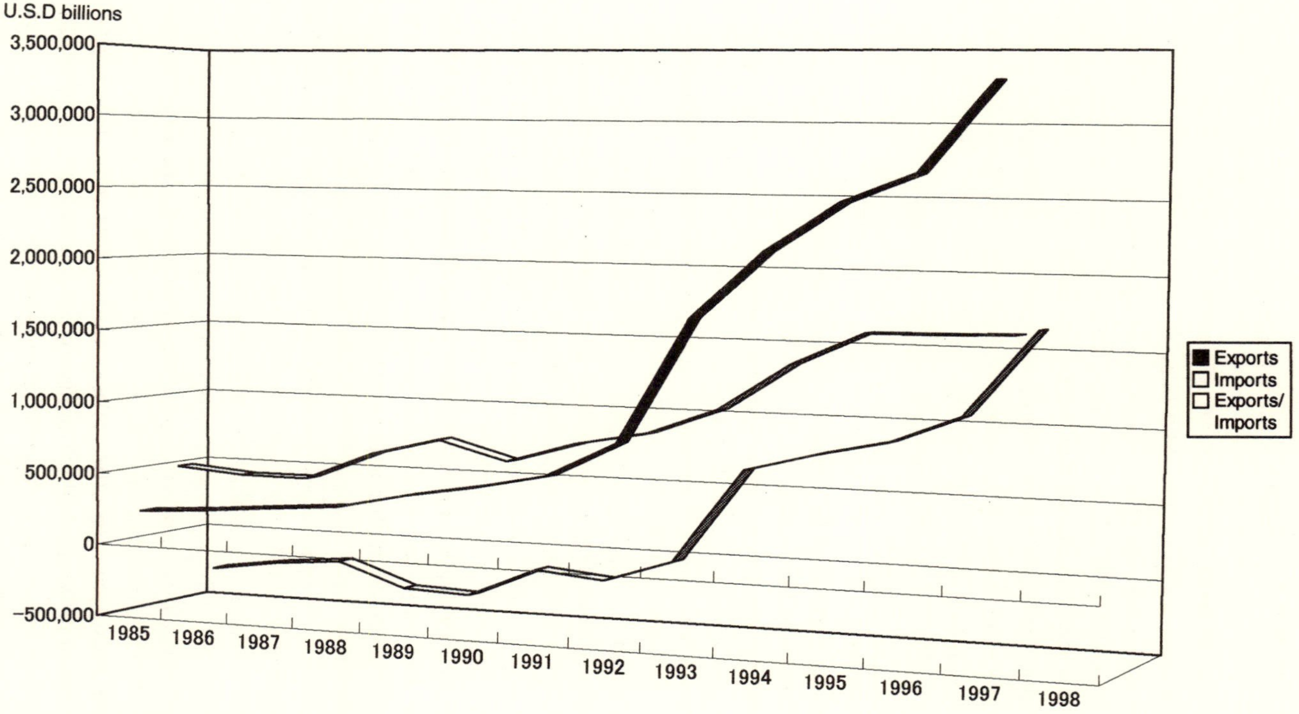

U.S.D billions

	Exports
■	Exports
□	Imports
□	Exports/ Imports

Source: State Statistical Bureau (various years).

Exhibit 6.2
U.S. Demands on China

- Eliminate tariffs on high-tech products over a five-year period*
- Eliminate tariffs on toys and furniture*
- Modify animal and plant health rules to accommodate the imports of wheat, citrus, and meat*
- Raise import quotas on state-traded commodities
- Raise auto import quota and loosen distribution regulations
- Lift ban on direct foreign investment and control of Telecom companies[+]
- Open the entire country to foreign insurers[+]
- Lower tariffs on agricultural products by 70 percent[+]
- Adhere to WTO rules on the scientific justification of blocking certain imports[+]
- Allow banks to enter domestic currency transactions, such as auto/car loans throughout the country[+]

---

*= already agreed; [+] = under negotiation.
Source: Compiled from Helene Cooper and Ian Johnson, *Wall Street Journal*, March 22, 1999, p. A2, and March 30, 1999, p. A2.

countries more for their markets and less for their political alliance and support against an enemy, the Soviet Union, which no longer exists. In either case, the United States has presented China with a list of demands that have been either fulfilled or are under negotiation (see Exhibit 6.2).

At any rate, China's concessions in anticipation of WTO membership have intensified competition for SOEs, a situation that is expected to deteriorate once China becomes a WTO member. Indeed, a World Bank study finds that major Chinese corporations will have difficulty surviving should a number of protectionism measures that seal them from foreign competition be eliminated. In fact, in spite of productivity gains, over 50 percent of SOEs run deficits financed by state-owned banks. But even those enterprises that run profits would not have been doing so if it were not for low or even interest-free loans by state banks, an issue to be further addressed below.

Worse, China's benefits from a WTO membership may not be as great as expected, because some of China's major exports continue to be subject to tariffs. Yang and Zhong, for instance, observe that China's major export textiles will continue to be subject to tariffs, even after WTO rules take full effect in 2005. "Although the multi-fibre Arrangement (MFA, which has regulated the world textile and clothing market through voluntary export restraints (VERs) for over two decades) is to be phased out by the year 2005, tariffs on textiles and clothing remain high in industrial markets."[3] Besides, a number of countries, including Japan, have begun to renegotiate bilateral agreements with China, placing quantitative restrictions on China's exports.

China's entry to world markets comes at a time when capitalism is stretching its geographical limits, a time when world markets are already crowded with too many products and competitors, namely the Asian and Latin American NIEs, countries that produce similar products, especially after the currency crisis. Compounding the problem of late arrival and crowded world markets is China's large volume of exports, which makes her corporations price makers rather than price takers, in direct competition with themselves. As Sato observes:

Another factor in the problems of Southeast Asia has been the rise of China as an export powerhouse which reduced smaller countries' competitiveness in exporting products. With the 1994 devaluation of the renminbi, China surpassed many of the Asian countries in its export competitiveness, causing excessive competition for export markets in the Asian region.[4]

China's heavy weight on world markets is particularly evident in industrial commodity markets, where China's SOEs hold a substantial share of world markets. "China has emerged as one of the most influential long-term factors in world commodity markets. . . . Day in and day out, its secrecy and the unpredictable production cycles of its half-command, half-market economy drive prices of a dozen of commodities"[5]

Internal pressures come from China's failure to develop a single integrated domestic market that would allow her companies to take advantage of the economies of scale as other countries, most notably Japan, did in the past. In spite of the progress the country has made in recent years, her domestic market remains a collection of separate local markets rather than a single integrated market. Poor infrastructure, for instance, constrains the physical integration of commodity markets, while low worker mobility constrains the integration of labor markets. Sharp income inequalities between the Southeast regions and the rest of the country create a two-tiered economy.

China's current failure to attain her full potential may be attributed to a number of factors, including low per capita income, persistent income inequalities, low

population density, high illiteracy rates, and poor physical market integration.
... China is a tale of two economies—that of the rapidly modernizing south-eastern coastal economy from Haina and Guandong to Liaoning, and that of a backward central-southwestern and northwestern economy from Guangxi to Xianjiang and Inner Mongolia.[6]

Internal pressures also come from China's inability to adjust inputs and outputs to changing market conditions and her incapability to innovate and create sustainable competitive advantages. Such inability and incapability in turn reflect the country's communist legacy that continues to hold the economy hostage to the vested interests of government bureaucrats and Communist Party leaders, who maintain their grip on the economy, especially on SOEs and the banking system, as discussed in the previous chapter.

China's inability and incapability to innovate have by default left volume expansion of conventional products as the sole competitive strategy. The country, for instance, consistently expanded its zinc production from 4.4 percent in 1980 to 10.9 percent in 1990 and 18.6 percent in 1997. Over the same period, China's tin production expanded from 7.9 percent to 18.4 percent and 31.3 percent.[7]

Based on imitation and volume rather than on innovation and quality, China's competitive strategy has resulted in the destruction of her export prices. Between 1985 and 1995, for instance, a period during which China experienced a nearly 40 percent devaluation of her currency, the export unit value of wrist watches dropped by 66 percent, the export unit value of clocks dropped by 47 percent, the export unit value of electric fans dropped by 44 percent, and the export unit value of dry cells dropped by 32 percent (see Exhibit 6.3). In fact, during this period, only one export commodity, cameras, escaped price destruction and even registered substantial price appreciation.

Price destruction caused by excess supply is not limited to exports; it extends to almost every product, as is reflected in excess business inventories and in a 1.9 percent decline in retail prices in February 1998, and in the decline in retail prices that fell from close to 16 percent in 1994 to less than 2 percent in 1998,[8] and were expected to fall to −2 percent in 1999.[9] In the words of Roberts et al., "Deflation is ravaging Chinese enterprises. These companies, most of them state-owned, have accumulated hundreds of billions of dollars in unused inventories."[10] Worse, excess supply extends to labor markets. In the mid-1990s, SOEs alone had an excess of 23 million workers, and if the 120 million under-

Exhibit 6.3
China's Export Unit Value (1985–1996)

Unit Value (1985=1)

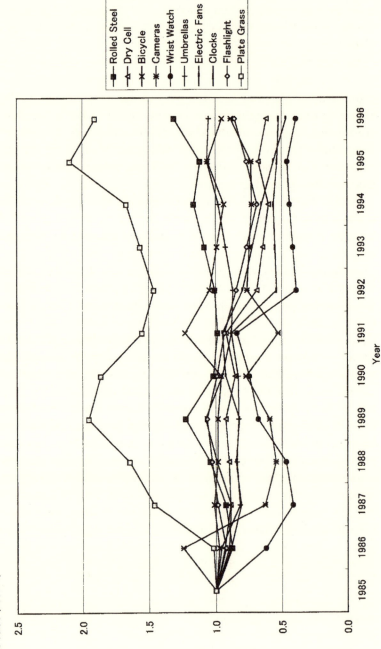

employed rural migrant workers are added, China's official unemployment rate of 3 percent jumps to close to 10 percent.[11] In fact, China's unemployment rate increased from 3.3 percent in 1993 to 8 percent in 1998.[12]

As expected, price destruction took its toll on one of the country's exports, especially after the Asian crisis. In 1998, for instance, China's exports fell to around 7 percent, one-third of the previous year's growth. Compounding the problem of slower export growth, the Asian crisis scared away foreign investors, making it difficult for its allying SOEs to raise capital through initial public offerings. By 1997, direct foreign investment had fallen to half of its 1995 size, while exports slowed down (see Exhibits 6.4 and 6.5).

With both exports and foreign investment slowing down, China's economic growth came down to earth. Indeed, economic growth declined from its 14 percent peak in 1993 to around 8 percent in 1999 (see Exhibit 6.6).

In short, China's lack of an expanding international and domestic frontier and her inability to innovate have taken their toll on her economy, most notably on her SOEs, which have been faced with declining profitability. Indeed, SOE profits declined from RMB80 billion in 1994 to RMB20 billion in 1998 (see Exhibit 6.7). With declining profits, SOEs continued to rely on state banks, both for short-term (working) capital and medium-term capital. Indeed, in 1997, close to 90 percent of state bank capital was allocated to finance the capital needs of SOEs (see Exhibit 6.8). Reflecting the heavy SOE borrowing from banks, the debt-to-equity ratio of some SOEs has exceeded 500. In practice, such a heavy debt burden means "that many of China's state-owned firms are insolvent—some cannot even cover their operating costs with their income."[13]

Worse, such loans were made at below deposit rates, turning the interest rate spread negative. Indeed, from April 1990 to January 1995, the gap between the average deposit rates and lending rates for ten-year loans ranged between −0.36 and −4.32 percentage points.[14]

The Chinese government sets many interest rates according to industrial or broader policy objectives rather than according to commercial ones, and the commercial banks are still obliged to carry the loans at the dictated rates. Moreover, the commercial banks' biggest burden is unrecoverable working capital loans to defray public enterprise losses.[15]

In addition, the country's economic slowdown has taken its toll on the central and provincial governments, which also turned to banks to fi-

Exhibit 6.4
Foreign Direct Investment in China (1995–1997)

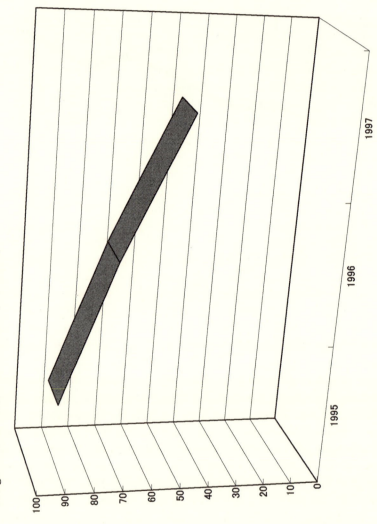

Source: State Statistical Bureau (various years).

Exhibit 6.5
China's Trade (1992–1997)

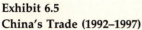

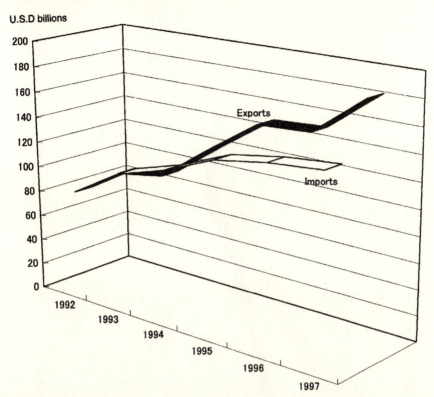

Source: State Statistical Bureau (various years).

nance their spending, an issue that will be further addressed in the next chapter.

Reflecting the increasing reliance of both SOEs and government on bank financing, when the economy slowed down, M2, a broad measure of money supply took off (see Exhibit 6.9). Such monetary expansion in turn fueled China's own economic bubble—Securities markets, both in Shanghai and in Hong Kong, soared. Between 1994 and 1997, for instance, the number of listed companies in the Shanghai and Shenzhen increased from 291 to 745, daily volume trade increased from $400 million to $1.65 billion; and market capitalization increased from $42.2 billion $211.2 billion.[16] Real estate prices also rose in Hong Kong, both before and after the Chinese takeover. In fact, a land auction that took place at the end of August 1997, less than two months after Hong Kong

Exhibit 6.6
Real GDP Growth (1994–1999)

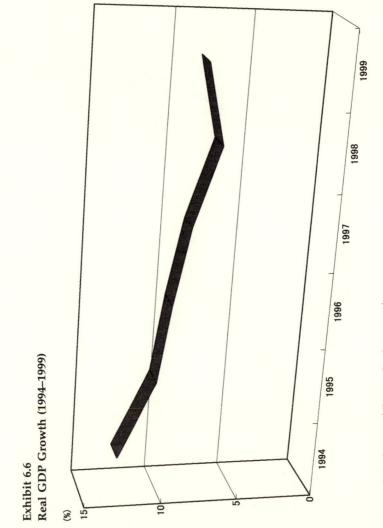

Source: State Statistical Bureau (various years).

Exhibit 6.7
SOE Profits (1994–1998)

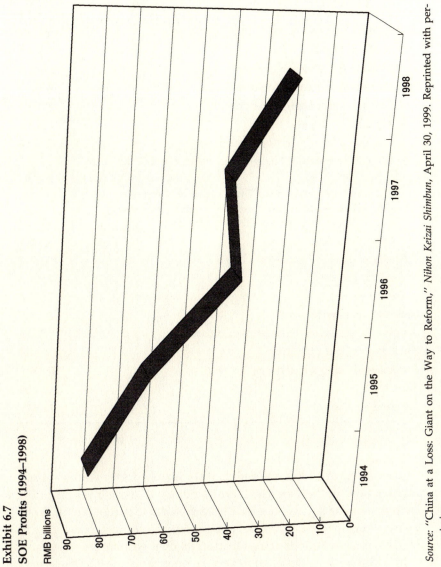

Source: "China at a Loss: Giant on the Way to Reform," *Nihon Keizai Shimbun*, April 30, 1999. Reprinted with permission.

139

Exhibit 6.8
Credit Funds Balance Sheet of State Bank User Funds in 1997

Item	1997
All Uses	965,008.1
Loans	74,914.1
Short-Term Loans	55,418.3
Loans to Industrial Enterprises	10,526.6
Loans to Commercial Enterprises	18,356.6
Loans to Construction Enterprises	1,591.1
Agricultural Loans	3,314.6
Loans to Urban Collective Enterprises	5,035.8
Loans to Individuals Engaged in Industrial and Commercial Business	386.7
Loans to Enterprises in the Three Forms of Ventures: Sino-Foreign Joint Ventures, Cooperative Enterprises, and Exclusively Foreign-Funded Enterprises	1,891.0
Other Short-Term Loans	8,315.9
Medium-Term and Long-Term Loans	15,468.7
Credit Loans	2,322.1
Other Loans	1,705.0
Securities and Investments	3,671.7
Assets in International Financial Institutions	534.4
Purchases of Gold and Silver	12.0
Purchases of Foreign Exchanges	13,467.2
Vault Cash	826.6
Government Debt	1,582.1

Source: State Statistical Bureau (various years).

was returned to China, yielded sharply higher prices. And as Japanese investors did in the 1980s with art paintings, Chinese investors are now snapping up antiques—one of the few assets that they are allowed to own—while their government is investing the country's trade surplus in U.S. government bonds rather than in its own economy.[17]

In addition, price destruction and the opening of the Chinese economy to world markets have created an entirely new world for banks, an uncertain environment manifested in the clash between central planners and market forces. Under central planning, supply created its own de-

Exhibit 6.9
Money Supply of China (1977–1995)

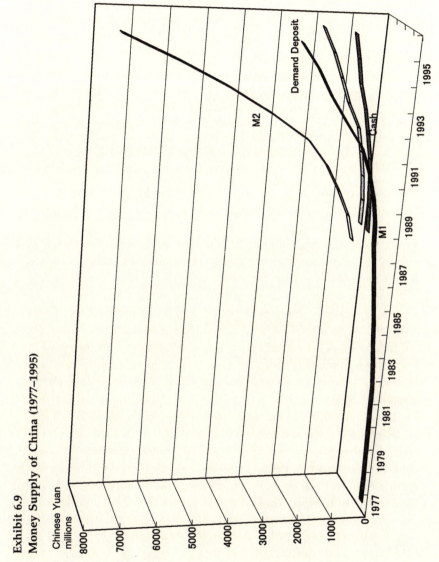

Source: International Monetary Fund.

mand, which in an attempt to keep the cost of living low was rationed at below market price, perhaps explaining the frequent shortages of commodities in China and other central planning countries. But as central planners eased their grip on the economy, as demand took precedence over supply, it became increasingly difficult for central planners to predict demand, which could explain the surplus created in a number of industries, with real estate being a case in point. According to the Housing Reform,

The middle class would buy the homes they rented from the government and so create a spending boom, with banks issuing mortgages and new homeowners refurbishing their flats. But the middle class hesitated to spend their savings on apartments they had been renting cheap, and the banks shied at the risk of lending to buyers. The expected housing market never materialized.[18]

This can explain the real estate glut and the growing apartment vacancies in China's Southeast regions, an issue that will be further addressed in the next chapter.

In short, by the mid-1990s, China's economy, which for almost two decades had been growing by leaps and bounds, was coming to a standstill and her industries and corporations began to taste the other side of globalization—increasing competition, price swings, and the increasing risk and uncertainty associated with them. For the first time, Chinese managers had to learn how to compete in a global economy, especially bank managers, who continued to lack the freedom, the incentive, and the expertise to manage risk. Yet they continued to lend to their corporate clients (SOEs) as though nothing had changed, piling up nonperforming loans.

In this sense, China's success in saving herself from the Asian contagion reflects more the low degree of integration of the Chinese economy to the global economy and less the subtle, intelligent Beijing policies. Further, this means that unlike other Asian countries, a full-blown banking crisis is ahead rather than behind the Chinese economy, which will be addressed in the next chapter.

NOTES

1. Quoted in *The Economist*, April 17, 1999.
2. See Arayama and Mourdoukoutas (1999), ch. 1.
3. Yang and Zhong (1998), p. 3.

4. Sato (1998), p. 374.

5. I. Johnson and T. Ewing, "China Is a Big Swing in Commodity Markets," *Wall Street Journal*, November 23, 1998, p. A18.

6. Arayama and Mourdoukoutas (1999), p. 32.

7. Ibid.

8. Smith (1994), p. R4.

9. I. Johnson, "China, With Economy Slowing, Renews Its Push to Join WTO," *Wall Street Journal*, June 4, 1999, p. A6.

10. D. Roberts, J. Barnathan, J. More, and S. Prasso, "China: What's Going Wrong?" *Business Week*, February 22, 1999.

11. *Asian Development Report* (1987), p. 49.

12. Saywell and Jiangsu (1999), p. 47.

13. Lardy (1996), p. 81.

14. Fry (1998), p. 96.

15. Brean (1998), p. 9.

16. Leggett (1998), p. R10.

17. Smith (1994).

18. Roberts et al., "China: What's Going Wrong?" p. 49.

Chapter 7

The Looming
Banking Crisis in China

As in Japan, the only big spender in China is the Government, which is pouring money into concrete, bricks and mortar for bridges, dams and other projects, even if they crumble thanks to hasty construction or corruption.

—Sheryl WuDunn[1]

The Chinese now see clearly that a domestic banking sector plagued with bad loans is a time bomb. An initial currency crisis, like a rapid depreciation of the exchange rate, can quickly become a pervasive domestic financial crisis, ruining both commercial and investment banks.

—Shang-Jin Wei and Richard J. Zeckhauser[2]

In most market economies when borrowers cannot meet their debt obligations for two consecutive months lenders call in the loans and eventually force the borrower to foreclose and liquidate the assets placed on collateral for the loan. And in most market economies, government regulators monitor closely the financial performance of thrifts, especially their reserves, shutting down the insolvent ones. In most market economies, banks screen prospective clients and set lending rates according to their ability to repay loans.

As a rule this is not the case in China, however, especially since 1995, when price destruction and slower economic growth worsened the economic conditions of SOEs. In an effort to keep SOEs afloat and preserve employment for millions, Chinese bureaucrats have been overtaken by growth hysteria, turning to infrastructure projects to make up for the slowdown in export growth and the shortfall in foreign investments. With eroding tax revenues, government bureaucrats have found monetary policy and banking credit in particular the sole vehicle of financing such projects. In fact, government bureaucrats have been ordering state banks to expand their credit to already-bankrupt SOEs by Western standards, precipitating rather than ending the banking crisis.

Arguing this proposition, this chapter takes a close look at the size of China's banking crisis and extends the discussion of the previous chapters to identify and elaborate on the factors that are fueling such a crisis—namely, the failure of banks to apply the principles of financial management, the slowdown in economic growth, the lack of a sound taxation system, excess liquidity, the lack of a sound fiscal system, the establishment of ITICs, an asset bubble, and the rapid deterioration of the situation of SOEs.

On February 17, 1999, Beijing shut down one of the best-known City International Trading Corporations (CITCs), the Guangdong International Trust Corporation (GITC). On June 23 of the same year, the executive vice governor of POB authorized the injection of 30 billion yuan to Guangdong Enterprises, the province investment subsidiary in Hong Kong.[3] On June 21, 1998, the Beijing government ordered the closure of the Hainan Development Bank, the first bank to fail since communist rule went into effect in 1949.

Though three isolated examples do not constitute sufficient evidence for a full-blown banking crisis in China, they point to a looming banking crisis as well as a number of foreign credit reports on the country's major banks. In October 1998, for instance, Thomson Bankwatch downgraded several Chinese banks, including major banks such as the Agricultural Bank, the Bank of China, and the Industrial and Commercial Bank of China (see Exhibit 7.1). A few months earlier, Moody's downgraded a number of ITICs, including the Fujan ITIC, the Shandong ITIC, and the Shanghai ITIC (see Exhibit 7.2). In fact, according to some estimates, at the end of 1998 Chinese banks had more than $200 billion in bad loans (29 percent of their outstanding loans) and were already bankrupt by Western standards.[4] Worse, non-performing assets were concentrated in the country's ten commercial banks and four state-run banks, which amounted to RMB1.6 trillion, or 25 percent of all outstanding loans.[5] In

Exhibit 7.1
Selected Bank Downgrades as of October 15, 1998

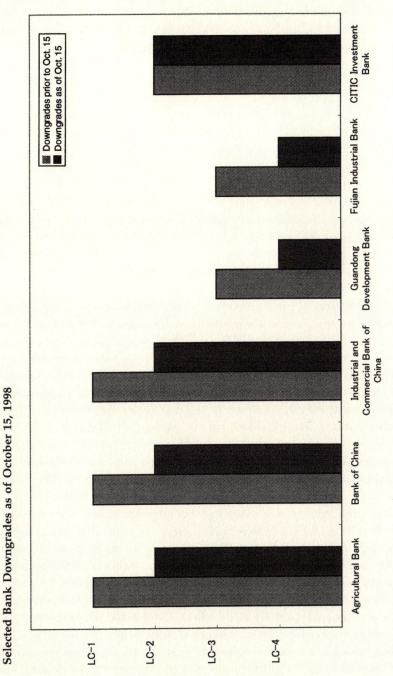

Source: Adapted from Thomson Bankwatch.

Exhibit 7.2
Moody's Credit Rating for Selected ITICs

Name of ITIC	Credit Rating
Fujan ITIC	Baa2
Shandong ITIC	Baa2
Shanghai ITIC	Baa2
Shenzen ITIC	Ba1
Tianjin ITIC	Ba1

Source: "China's ITICs Feel the Heat from Moody's," *Euroweek,* 1998, p. 14.

fact, according to some estimates, "These loans have gone to loss-making state enterprises and to politically connected businessmen rather than to the best projects."[6] When such loans to SOEs are combined with subsidies and transfers from the banking system, they account for 5 percent of GDP.[7]

In this sense, China's banking crisis is not reflected in the amount of non-performing assets accumulated in the books of Chinese banks alone; they are in the books of SOEs and their subsidiaries, which are often created for the purpose of hiding them.[8] Well-known corporations such as Cosco Group Ltd., Shanghai Industrial Investment, and Guandong Enterprises Ltd. carry debt loads comparable to those of Thai and Korean firms (see Exhibit 7.3). In fact, "a half dozen provincial-owned companies have missed foreign debt-payments. At least a half dozen more companies in the province have defaulted on domestic bonds."[9] The list of such companies include well-known names such as Maoming Quinghua Co. and the Huizhou Yinshan Development Co. (see Exhibit 7.4). After all, as discussed in the previous chapters, SOEs and government banks continue to function as government departments rather than as separate entities in a lender-borrower relationship, as is the case in market economies. Within this function, Chinese banks are the primary financiers of the country's budget, especially in recent years. In 1996, for instance, banks financed close to 86 percent of the country's deficit.[10]

Regardless of how non-performing assets are measured and reported, China's looming banking crisis reflects the rise and fall of abacus banking and the deliberate efforts of national, provincial, and local bureaucrats and bankers to preserve economic growth and the status quo and their failure to apply the principles of risk management in evaluating invest-

Exhibit 7.3

Debt-to-Equity Ratios of the Mainland Parents of Some Prominent Hong Kong "Red Chips" as of December 31, 1997

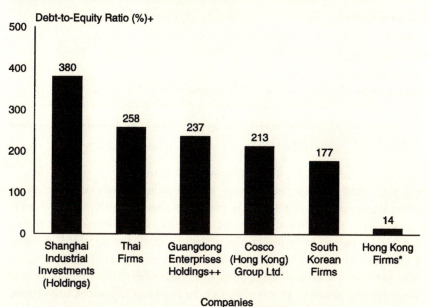

*= estimate; + = early 1998; ++ = as of July 30, 1997.

Source: Adapted from Erik Guyot, "Major Chinese Firms Carry Debt Loads on a Par with Currency-Crisis Victims," *Wall Street Journal*, April 21, 1998, p. A19.

ment alternatives. Specifically, China's looming banking crisis is fueled by the combination of a number of factors:

- The failure of banks to apply the principles of risk management to evaluate alternatives.
- The slow down in economic growth.
- The lack of a sound taxation system and fiscal policy that leaves monetary policy the sole vehicle of expansionary policy, even if that means a negative interest rate spread for state banks.
- Excess liquidity created by state banks in support of the efforts of provincial and local governments to preserve growth and employment in SOEs and TVEs.
- The establishment of ITICs and credit collectives serving as the vehicles of financing provincial and local projects.
- The asset bubble fueled by excessive spending financed by state banks and ITICs.

Exhibit 7.4
Corporations that Missed Bond Payments in 1999

Maoming Quinghua Co.

Huizhou Yinshan Development Co.

Foshan Fenjiang Industrial Co.

East River Power Co.

Yanjang Hi-tech Base Construction Development Corp.

Source: Compiled from C. Smith and K. Leggett, "Chinese Face More Defaults by State
Firms," *Wall Street Journal,* February 13, 1999, p. A18.

In market economies, where economic resources are privately owned
and managed, business capacity expansion is normally demand-driven.
New investment projects begin with the identification of new demands,
proceed with feasibility studies and financing, and end with the hiring
of relevant inputs for their implementation. Both the corporations that
pursue the investment projects and the bankers who eventually finance
them evaluate investment alternatives according to the principles of risk
management. Besides, in market economies, both investors and banks
are accountable for the losses that may occur due to poor judgment or
reckless choices.

This is not the case in China, however, where economic resources are
government-owned and managed, and business capacity expansion is
supply-driven. In this system, central planning units, namely SOEs and
TVEs, are first assigned economic inputs and then they secure financing
and search for market opportunities. In this sense, SOE and TVE managers who pursue investment opportunities and the bank managers who
finance them lack the freedom, the incentives, and the expertise to evaluate investment alternatives, and they are not accountable for losses due
to poor judgment, as is the case in the market economies. In addition,
the primary objective of central planning is the full rather than the efficient deployment of economic resources. Often SOEs and TVEs pursue
projects for the sole purpose of providing employment and income to
their labor force rather than satisfying efficiently and effectively consumer demands. As Zhang puts it,

In a free market banks would direct savings into profitable investments. Under
Beijing they are being consumed by inefficient state enterprises. And I mean
consumed. These state dinosaurs are using up billions of dollars of capital that

would have been employed elsewhere, adding to China's capital structure and raising future living standards."[11]

Supporting and reinforcing SOEs' expansion bias is their privileged treatment by state banks. According to Lu and Yu,

Privileged access to easy and low-cost credit encourages state-owned enterprises to aggressively expand borrowing from banks, with little concern for interest costs and investment risks. Despite this preferential treatment, their contribution to total industrial output declined from 78 percent in 1978 to 43 percent in 1993, yet their borrowing still accounts for over 80 percent of total bank credits.[12]

Chinese bank managers' lack of freedom and expertise to allocate investment funds according to the principles of risk management has resulted in a duplication of economic projects and a concentration of such projects to a few regions and to the sectors prone to bubbles. This is particularly the case in the aftermath of the Asian crisis, when economic growth slowed down substantially and it became increasingly difficult for SOEs to maintain staff levels or to provide employment for newcomers. Government bureaucrats were taken by growth hysteria, manifested in a massive infrastructure spending as an alternative source of growth. Indeed, in 1998, almost two-thirds of the country's economic growth came from infrastructure spending. In this sense, China follows in Japan's footsteps, with one difference. In contrast to Japan, China lacks the tax revenues and the proper mechanisms to enforce tax collection, to keep tax revenues at the level of economic growth, and to finance such projects. "An ineffective tax system is to blame for China's delicate finances. Poor enforcement means tax collectors haven't been able to tap the country's explosive economic growth."[13] Factored in the pricing of the SOE and TVE products, rather than based on income, value-added tax (VAT), or sales, the Chinese government tax base has been eroding rather than expanding.[14] Between 1970 and 1995, the gross output value of the Chinese industry rose by over 40 times, while tax revenues rose by less than under 10 times (see Exhibit 7.5).

The erosion of China's tax base by default leaves monetary expansion and bank lending (seigniorage income) as the sole alternative of financing government spending and preserving economic growth, at the expense of economic reforms, even if such monetary expansion means a negative interest rate spread for banks.[15]

Exhibit 7.5

Government Revenues, Expenditures, and Debt Incurred (1970–1995)

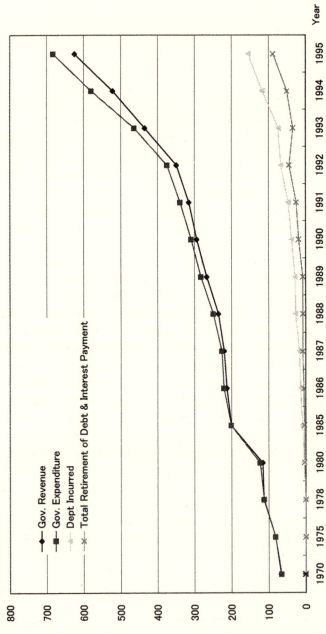

Chinese Yuan billions

The interest rate policies of the Chinese government bears watching for it is a sure signal of the commitment of the government for free market reforms. One alarming development in the economic scene is the decision to increase deposit rates and decrease lending rates. This development, coupled with a directive to Chinese banks by the government to lend to regional governments and infrastructure projects, is a clear indication of the Chinese government's decision to prioritize economic growth over economic reform.[16]

It comes as no surprise, therefore, that bank financing of the government deficit increased from 4 percent in 1985 to 85.7 percent in 1996.[17] Since the beginning of the Asian crisis, the BOC (1) has slashed official lending rates five times and ordered banks to raise lending rates; (2) has raised annual loan upper limits for Chinese banks from RMB 900 billion ($108.7 billion) to RMB 1 trillion; and (3) has lowered the reserve requirements of banks from 13 percent to 8 percent.[18] Reflecting this shift in monetary policy, the proportion of loans to bank assets has remained high compared to the United States, and has even increased for the 1994–1997 period (see Exhibits 7.6 and 7.7). Loans to SOEs have zoomed, from a few billion yuan in 1978 to 5 trillion in 1996. And by Western accounting standards, many SOEs and the banks that finance them have a negative net worth. In fact, as discussed in the previous chapter, for the 1990–1995 period the interest rate spread turned negative.

Accommodating China's efforts to expand liquidity is the creation of credit collectives and ITICs. Introduced in the 1980s as separate state bank departments or bank subsidiaries and affiliates, ITICs were engaged in the risk-free "agency business," that is, taking entrusted deposits from institutional sources for non-discretionary loans and investments at the discretion of the client. In this capacity, ITICs were supposed to assist state banks in coping with the rapid growth in lending that characterized that period. It did not take long, however, before these institutions came under the control of provincial and local governments and expanded from risk-free entrusted deposit activities to high-risk financing activities. ITICs raised a huge amount of funds both domestically and internationally for the financing of smaller, less reputable local corporations that would not have had access to organized capital markets.

These institutions have been able to circumvent the constraints under which the traditional financial system operates: they have chosen borrowers and projects outside the state's Credit Plan, they have enjoyed greater discretion on the rates

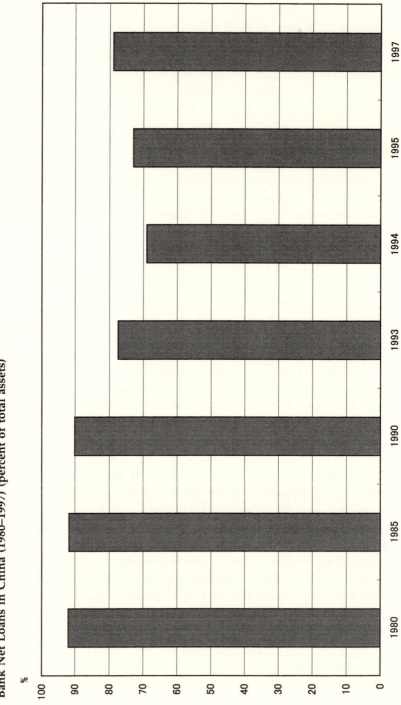

Exhibit 7.6
Bank Net Loans in China (1980–1997) (percent of total assets)

Exhibit 7.7
Bank Net Loans in the United States (1980–1995) (percent of total assets)

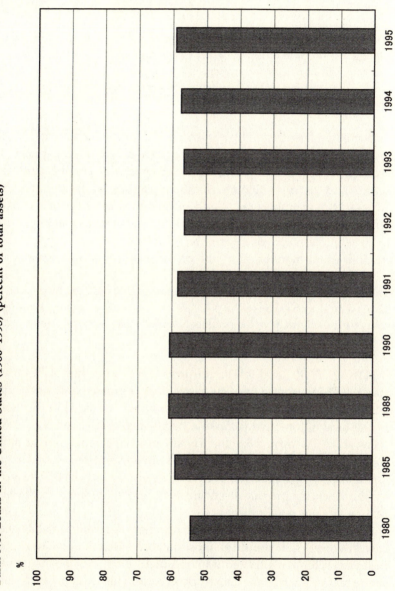

and terms they offer for lending and have provided a range of services not offered by banks. They also had access to funding other than conventional deposits and have provided stimulating competition to traditional financial institutions.[19]

ITICS amassed huge amounts of funds both in the domestic and in foreign markets for the purpose of financing provincial and local projects such as housing and commercial real estate projects. ITICs played an important role. They provided funds to China's less reputable companies that wouldn't have access to domestic equity markets and foreign banks.[20]

Owned and controlled by provincial and local governments, which are often at odds with Beijing over the direction of economic policy, ITICs escaped from regulation and central government control, turning into some kind of discretionary, hidden reserves of local governments. "These TICs were born as a kind of hidden reserve for provincial governments. They were forced by local governments to make investments in local projects or give loans to local enterprises. They lacked self-discipline and monitoring by the central bank."[21] In this sense,

Their role in China's financial system has been characterized by a series of cyclical swings, with expansion and diversification being encouraged during cyclical upturns, only to have their numbers, growth and scope of activity tightened during more strained economic periods.[22]

SITICO, TITIC, and ZITIC are three cases in point. SITICO, for instance, is 85 percent owned by the Shanghai municipality and functions as a development bank in the Shanghai region, engaged in the financing of the local automotive company, hotels, real estate, and land development. TITIC is owned by the Tianjin municipal government and also functions as a local development bank, financing technology companies and real estate projects, and even trading unlisted stocks. ZITIC is owned by the Zhejiang provincial government and is engaged in the leasing, real estate, and hotel business.

Escaping the close scrutiny of government regulators, as has been the case in other Asian countries, most notably with their counterparts *jusen* in Japan, ITICs have turned into speculative vehicles, financing bubble-prone sectors such as the construction sector (see Exhibit 7.8). In fact, the signs of over-construction are evident across China's major cities, where many buildings are unfinished and abandoned, especially in Shanghai, where over 50 percent of buildings are vacant.[23] According to Lardy,

Exhibit 7.8
Production, Employment, and Establishments in the Construction Sector in China (1981–1996)

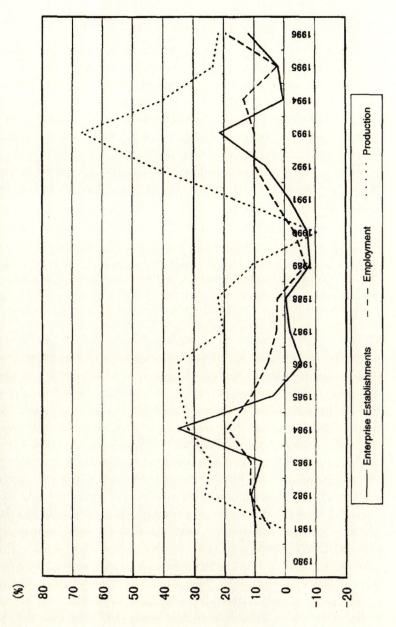

By the mid-1990's, far too much had been built. Beijing, Shanghai, and Shenzhen appear to have the highest concentrations of unleased luxury villas and town-houses and first-class office space, but many smaller cities, ranging from Haiku on Hainan island to Beihai in Guangxi, have a significant problem of over-building.[24]

China's excess capacity is also reflected in excessive duplication of ec-onomic activity (i.e., the establishment of companies producing similar products, just for the sake of creating employment for the excess labor). "Companies built too many office buildings, started too many factories and borrowed money during the boom years."[25] In fact, in 1997, the Chinese government openly admitted that about half of its industrial product factories ran at 60 percent capacity.

In short, as was the case in Japan, China's banking crisis is the result of the rise and fall of abacus banking strategy. An editorial in *Euroweek* stated that

Daunting difficulties of restructuring the country's loss-making state owned en-terprises and increasing unemployment are straining the financial resources of China's central and local governments and this weakens their ability to support the ITICs that they control.[26]

Hainan Development Bank is a good example of the rise and fall of abacus banking in China. The bank rose along with the economic growth of the Hainan province and also fell along with it. GITIC is another case in point. When the economy grew, the province was in a position to borrow heavily, both in domestic and international markets. "Guang-dong became a state within a state, a political fiefdom run by local lead-ers who paid lip service to Beijing."[27] Without proper feasibility studies to evaluate the alternatives of economic resources, the province poured billions of dollars into small-town airports, dams, and commercial real estate that were never utilized, especially as the economy slowed down. Consider Zhuhai's international airport. Costing $400 million to build, it handles less than a half dozen domestic flights a week, and therefore is grossly underutilized.[28]

China's efforts to preserve growth in coastal provinces that formerly relied heavily on exports for their prosperity are reflected in the unequal growth of state bank loans. State bank loan growth to coastal areas, for instance, increased from close to 20 percent in 1990 to around 44 percent in 1994, while loan growth in other areas of the country dropped from around 24 percent in 1990 to around −1 percent (see Exhibit 7.9).

At this point, one may raise two important questions. How did Chinese banks survive on a negative interest rate spread? Why have monetary expansion and excess liquidity not created hyperinflation? There are two reasons, according to Fry.[29] First, because of the issuance of bank bonds, which in essence have reduced banks' net worth. Indeed, bond issues increased, from about $15 billion in 1993 to $38 billion in 1999.[30] Second, because of the preservation of one of the conditions of abacus banking—the regulation of financial markets and interest rates—which maintained a wide margin between demand deposits and time deposits, allowing banks to continue to derive seigniorage income. According to Kime,

The Chinese government continues to regulate closely all deposit and lending rates and to limit the financial instruments available to the public. In addition, by insuring that China's state-owned banks maintain a near monopoly over the economy's financial resources, the government has forced the public to hold its financial wealth in the form of either non-interest earning currency or in state-bank deposits that sometimes earn negative real rates of return.[31]

In fact, interest rate controls and financial regulation are the "Achilles' heel" of the Chinese banking system. One must therefore understand China's reluctance to deregulate her financial markets, especially interest rates. Should such deregulation take place and the gap between short-term rates and long-term rates narrow, Chinese banks would no longer survive on seigniorage income, declaring insolvency, which was the case with some of their Japanese and Southeast counterparts in the 1970s and the 1980s.

Once again, China faces a dilemma—preserve her financial regulation, risking her integration into the global economy, or proceed with deregulation and risk a full-scale banking crisis that would dwarf that of Japan and other Asian countries.

To sum up, as was the case in Japan and other Asian countries, China's looming banking crisis reflects excess liquidity and excess capacity, fueled by an overexpansion that created both a commodity and an asset bubble. But unlike the other Asian countries and Japan, China's bubble is government-driven. It reflects the desperate attempts of Beijing and provincial governments to hold onto the old system of central planning that allocates resources according to the principles of central planning

Exhibit 7.9
Annual Growth Rate of Loans in State-Owned Banks by Region (1990–1994)

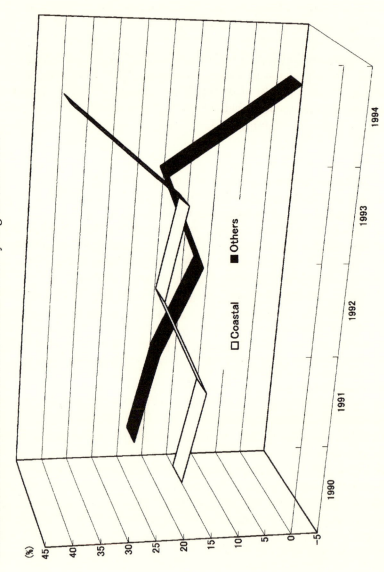

Source: Adapted from China Finance Society (various years).

rather than according to the principles of efficiency and risk management. China's banking crisis further reflects the clash between the two opposing forces—the concentric forces that pull it toward centralization and the planning and centrifugal forces that pull it toward market forces—a conflict between those who support inefficient SOEs and those who support private-owned enterprises:

There is still an inherent conflict in China between a country committed to propping up its inefficient and loss-making enterprises with free government handouts and via the banks and one which is supposed to be committed to the advancement of market forces.[32]

NOTES

1. WuDunn (1998).
2. Wei and Zeckhauser (1998).
3. Smith and Leggett (1999), p. A18.
4. "China: Asia's Next Casualty," *Business Week* (editorial), December 15, 1997. See also The Economist Intelligence Unit, "Financing Foreign Operations in China" (June 1997), p. 28, and I. Johnson, "China Plans to Close Trust Companies in Crackdown," *Wall Street Journal*, January 7, 1998.
5. Gilley, "Breaking the Bank," *Far Eastern Review*, July 16, 1998, pp. 66–68.
6. Ibid., p. 68.
7. Fry (1998), p. 93.
8. In fact, as was the case in Japan, non-performing loans are often buried in SOE subsidiaries set up for this purpose or not even recorded at all.
9. Smith and Leggett (1999), p. A17.
10. Brean (1998), p. 8.
11. Zhang (1998), p. 1.
12. Lu and Yu (1998), p. 161.
13. I. Johnson, "China Calls for More Spending to Avoid Recession," *Wall Street Journal*, March 4, 1999, p. A9.
14. In the mid-1980s, China introduced both a corporate tax and a VAT tax, but given the ownership structure of the SOEs, it has not produced the expected results. For a detail discussion see Hay et al. (1994).
15. In fact, as it is often argued in the economic literature, a trade-off exists between seigniorage income created by issuing currency and the ability of governments to raise taxes (see Fry 1998).
16. C. Lo, "China Utilizes Its Banks, Choosing Growth over Reform," *The Asian Wall Street Journal Weekly*, Vol. 20, No. 30, July 27, 1998, p. 16.
17. Brean (1998), p. 8.
18. H. Sender, "Floods of Money," *Far Eastern Review*, October 1, 1998, p. 58.

19. Kumar et al. (1998), p. 1.

20. B. G. Knecht, "China's Big Trusts Teeter on Extinction's Edge," *Wall Street Journal*, November 6, 1998, p. A10.

21. H. Saywell, "Tic Fever," *Far Eastern Economic Review*, October 28, 1998, p. 54.

22. Kumar et al. (1998), p. 3.

23. A. Tanzer, "The Shanghai Bubble," *Forbes*, April 20, 1998, p. 48.

24. Nicholas Lardy, "China and the Asian Contagion," *Foreign Affairs*, Vol. 77, No. 4 (July–August 1998), pp. 78–88.

25. C. S. Smith, "Once Wealthy Guangdong Is Now Riddled with Debt," *Wall Street Journal*, February 23, 1999, p. A17.

26. "China's ITICs Feel the Heat from Moody's," *Euroweek* (editorial), January 30, 1998, p. 14.

27. Smith, "Once Wealthy Guangdong Is Now Riddled with Debt," p. A17.

28. Ibid., p. A17.

29. Fry (1998).

30. Johnson, "China Calls for More Spending to Avoid Recession," p. A9.

31. Kime (1998), p. 14.

32. "China's Economy: Red Alert," *The Economist* (editorial), October 24, 1998, pp. 23–26.

Chapter 8

Conclusions

The revolutionary idea that defines the boundary between modern
times and the past is the mastery of risk; the notion that the future
is more than a whim of the gods and that men and women are not
passive before nature.

—Peter Bernstein[1]

Revolutionary ideas are not always popular, especially for those who
find complacency and comfort with the status quo, those who believe
that the future will be just a replica of the past and the present.

For several decades, the mastery of risk was an unpopular, irrelevant
idea among Japanese and Chinese bankers, who found comfort and complacency in a fast-growing economy and government regulation (Japan)
or government ownership (China), an environment that turned banking
into a routine accounting system, an abacus operation procedure. Every
year was another growth year under cozy government protection, bringing more of the same business, more deposits, more corporate loans, and
more profits. Like bread dough in the oven, banks could earn seigniorage
income simply by waiting, by riding along an uphill, safe ride rather
than by venturing into new business territory.

In the 1990s, the mastery of risk became popular or at least relevant
among Japanese and Chinese bankers, who could no longer find comfort

and complacency in a slow-growing and less-regulated environment. Every year was no longer a growth year under government protection, and every year did not bring more of the same business, but different, less predictable business and non-performing assets. Like it or not, Japanese and Chinese bankers have come up against the "boundary" that separates the old from the new times, the passive acceptance of destiny from the mastery of risk, a boundary that they have yet to cross.

An inquiry into the Japanese and Chinese banking crises, this book searches for answers to such crises beyond non-performing assets to the economic environment, "the regime," as Mancur Olson would have put it, which sets the parameters of the game and nurtures management behavior. In particular, this book argues that an American-style rescue package is not sufficient to end the Japanese banking crisis or to avert the looming Chinese crisis because these crises are rooted in the very nature of the Japanese and Chinese economies that deprive bank managers of the freedom, the ability, and the incentives to master traditional and non-traditional banking risks. Accustomed to high growth and tight government regulation, or outright ownership that limited competition (Japan) or rationed credit (China), and in effect controlled management behavior, Japanese and Chinese bankers have grown up as abacus bankers, masters of the abacus or the computer just for the monitoring of money flows rather than for managing risks.

As masters of the abacus, Japanese and Chinese bankers relied on passive-volume lending and seigniorage income for their survival and prosperity. This was particularly true during the high-growth eras (1950–1989 for Japan and 1978–1993 for China), when robust economic growth boosted personal income and savings and provided a steady flow of deposits to the banking system, while government regulation limited traditional and non-traditional banking risks. Bank deposits were in turn channeled to the large corporate sectors of the two countries, creating seigniorage income and providing steady welfare to their labor force at the same time.

Relying on volume lending and functioning as welfare agencies rather than as true banks, Japanese managers by nature and Chinese managers by social rule were possessed by a mass hysteria, rushing to load and then unload assets indiscriminately, causing wild price gyrations and financial crises. As the economy expanded, against every principle of risk management, Japanese and Chinese bankers financed investments in overvalued real estate, equities, art, and other objects of speculation. As the economy contracted, Chinese and Japanese bankers in particular faced piles of non-performing assets and a genuine task to reckon with—learning to behave as true bankers, that is, to manage traditional and non-traditional risks, a problem that takes much longer to solve than unloading non-performing assets.

Arguing these points in more detail, this discussion advanced in two parts. Upon reviewing Japan's postwar model of export-led industrialization and economic experience, Part I of this book identified and elaborated on the conditions that contributed to the rise and fall of abacus banking and the banking crisis that followed. Upon reviewing China's postwar economic experience, especially the 1978 economic reforms, Part II of this book addressed the rise and fall of abacus banking in China and the looming banking crisis in the offing.

Focusing on the "extended high-growth" era (1950–1989), Chapter 2 argued that robust, export-led economic growth and tight government regulation built a sense of complacency among Japanese bankers, a feeling of a secure, prosperous world to be conquered without any special effort, a subtle risk management strategy. Steady economic growth allowed banks to progress in tandem and to compete on high-volume, low-profit-margin lending, taking a steady share of an ever-larger pie. Exchange rate controls limited foreign currency risks. Government protection from foreign competition and the bailing out of individual corporations limited systemic or aggregate risk. BOJ overlending in essence eliminated liquidity risk. Long-term and *keiretsu* relations between banks and their clients and rising asset values virtually eliminated individual risks. An "escorted convoy"-style MOF banking regulation system that protected banks from foreign and domestic competition further limited systemic credit risk.

A steady cash flow and a low-risk lending environment reduced Japanese banking to an accounting system, a gatekeeper of the river flow of funds from bank lenders (depositors) to bank borrowers (large corporations). Along the river flow, banks' profits could climb steadily and risk-free, just by appropriating the difference between loan interest and deposit interest. Besides, as members of *keiretsu* groups and functioning within the *Gosou-sendan Houshiki* (the "escorted convoy" system), bank managers had little freedom to manage their portfolios according to the principles of profit maximization and credit risk management.

Japan's rapid postwar, export-led industrialization and cozy government and *keiretsu* relations were not destined to last forever. Under external and internal pressures, the Japanese economy began to open its markets to domestic and foreign competition, turning the banking environment from a certain to an uncertain world. Elaborating on this major shift in the Japanese banking environment, Chapter 3 argued that a negative interest rate spread, a shift of corporate financing from bank loans to equity, the erosion of *keiretsu* relations, the slowing of economic growth and savings, and asset deflation turned banking from a routine, passive operation to an active risk management operation that could no longer be handled by the abacus or even the ATM machines that began to replace it.

Specifically, after the 1985 Plaza Accord, banks faced an uncertain, risky world:

- The lifting of exchange rate controls increased currency risks.
- The lifting of trade protectionism raised systemic credit risks.
- The abandonment of the policy of overlending by the BOJ raised liquidity risks.
- The disbanding of the "escorted convoy"-style banking regulation system no longer protected banks from internal and external competition, further raising systemic credit risks.
- The erosion of *keiretsu* relations and the decline in asset values, especially land values, raised individual risks.
- The slowdown in economic growth undermined the thin interest rate profit margin–large-volume lending strategy and *bogai*, the "detour" or cover-up of short-term losses.

Though gradual, the shift from a low-risk environment to a high-risk environment brought banks in a speculative frenzy that took them to the summit and then all the way to the bottom of the world banking system. Specifically, the yen appreciation, financial liberalization, and the monetary easing that followed the Plaza Accord had a contradictory impact on Japanese banks. On the one hand, expansionary monetary policy increased liquidity and fueled economic growth and asset inflation, expanding bank opportunities at reduced risks. On the other hand, financial deregulation intensified competition between banks and money market mutual funds and raised deposit interest rates, driving the interest rate spread negative, especially during the bubble years. In addition, rising corporate profits and a stronger yen allowed large corporations to raise funds internally or in the Eurobond and equity markets. Many of the country's largest corporations would issue equity or debt not for the purpose of financing their investment needs but in order to add excess capacity or deposit it in banks, taking advantage of the high interest rates.

The yen appreciation, financial deregulation, and hyperliquidity provided the funds, and deregulation provided the opportunity and the incentive for engaging banks in speculative activities. Caught in excess liquidity, a negative interest rate spread, and a declining demand for low-risk corporate loans, banks began to search for new clients in the high-risk small- and medium-sized corporations, real estate, and any other investment opportunity opened up by deregulation. Hyperliquidity and government deregulation prompted a restructuring of banks' balance sheets, increasing their exposure to traditional and non-traditional banking risks.

Elaborating on this shift in banking strategy, Chapter 4 argued that the Japanese banking crisis is the result of the rise and fall of the strategy of abacus banking. Nurtured in an environment of fast economic growth, *keiretsu* relations, and tight government regulation, Japanese bankers lack the ability, the incentives, and the skills to manage funds in a risky environment. Finding themselves with excess liquidity, Japanese banks either directly or indirectly (through the *jusen*) extended credit to *Gene-con* and other investors based on inflated bubble values rather than on economic fundamentals. So when the bubble burst and asset prices declined, banks ended up with non-performing assets. In this sense, the Japanese banking crisis reflects the failure of the entire Japanese system rather than the failure of individual banks, as was the case with the savings and loans crisis in the United States in the 1980s.

As was the case in Japan, easy access to Western markets and vigorous economic growth reinforced a sense of complacency among Chinese government bureaucrats and corporate managers, especially among bank managers, an issue addressed in Chapter 5. As long as the economy grew and domestic markets were sealed from competition and the risks and uncertainty associated with it, China could reap the benefits of both a closed, centrally planned economy and an open market economy. Chinese corporations could expand their presence in world markets without substantial concessions to opening their own markets to the products and businesses of other countries. Chinese bureaucrats and corporate managers believed that they could succeed in a global economy through imitation rather than innovation, without adjusting their inputs and outputs to changing demand and supply conditions.

The Chinese banking industry has always been a tightly regulated one, especially during the early communist era, when banks constituted government departments within a central plan that determined how credit should be allocated among sectors and corporations. But even in the later communist era, after the 1978 reforms, banks by and large continued to be owned and controlled by the government, and bank managers continued to function as government accountants, monitoring the money flows between households and government departments, rather than acting as true bank managers. As was the case with Japanese banks, Chinese banks could survive and prosper through volume lending and seigniorage income rather than through active asset management. This was particularly true in the late 1980s and the early 1990s, when robust economic growth boosted savings and lending to SOEs.

By the mid-1990s, as globalization began to show its dark side of crowded markets and declining prices, Chinese corporations found it increasingly difficult to compete in world markets on imitation alone, an issue addressed in Chapter 6. With the country's surplus with the rest of the world (and the United States in particular) soaring, and with the pressure to open up her domestic markets to foreign products, and with competition intensifying, Chinese managers discovered that competing in global markets takes more than imitation. It takes an environment conducive to creativity rather than conformity, an environment that does not blend well with central planning and abacus banking.

By the late 1990s in the Chinese economy, exports, one of the growth engines of the economy, had stalled, especially after the rapid devaluation of Southeast Asian currencies. Foreign investment, another growth engine, had also stalled, depriving Chinese corporations of much-needed foreign capital and technology. And as those two sectors of the economy stalled so did the country's economic growth, making it more difficult for banks' major clients (SOEs) to repay their loans.

In most market economies, banks would have called in their loans, forcing those clients to bankruptcy, but not in China. In an attempt to preserve the "iron bowl" of the working class and their own vested interests, Chinese bureaucrats ordered banks to expand rather than cut credit to SOEs. This meant that instead of addressing a looming banking crisis, China postponed and precipitated it.

Elaborating on China's looming banking crisis, Chapter 7 argued that, as was true in Japan and in other Asian countries, China's banking crisis reflects excess liquidity and excess capacity, manifested in commodity and asset bubbles. But unlike the other Asian countries and Japan, China's bubble is government-driven. It reflects the deliberate attempts of Beijing and provincial governments to save the old system of central planning that allocates resources according to the priorities of government bureaucrats rather than according to the principles of efficiency and risk management. China's banking crisis further reflects the clash between the two opposing forces—the concentric forces that pull it toward centralization and the planning and centrifugal forces that pull it toward market economies—a conflict between the proponents of inefficient SOEs and the proponents of private-owned enterprises.

In brief, Japan's prolonged banking crisis and China's looming banking crisis demonstrate the limitations of policies that deal just with nonperforming assets. The two crises show the difficulty that Japan, China, and the Asian economies in general had in integrating into the global economy and dealing with the risks and uncertainties brought about by the intensification of competition. Such difficulty in turn stems from the approach that Asian countries take toward globalization—drastically different from that of the United States—which continues to emphasize social over individual values, relations over market efficiency, and evolution over revolution.

Does this mean that the United States will continue to lead and Asian countries will continue to follow in the globalization race? Are the United States and Asia heading toward an economic clash? We would rather not give in to the temptation of speculating about the fortunes or the misfortunes gods save for the future of nations. Instead, we join the growing chorus of those who raise concerns about the fragility of an interdependent world economy and the banking industry in particular, a world where the economic problems of one country become the economic problems of every country, especially if that economy is the lynchpin of world economy, as is true in Japan and China.

NOTE

1. Bernstein (1998).

Selected Bibliography

Adams, F.M.T., and Hoshii, I. 1972. *A Financial History of the New Japan*. Tokyo: Kodansha International.

"After the Cut: Japanese Interest Rates." 1993. *The Economist*, September 11.

Allen, G. C. 1990. *Modern Japan and Its Problems*. London: Athlone.

Arayama, Y., and Mourdoukoutas, P. 1999. *China Against Herself: Innovation or Imitation in Global Business?* Westport, CT: Quorum Books.

Arnold, W. 1998. "Japan's Daiwa, Trailing Technology, Turns to IBM." *Wall Street Journal*, October 19.

"As Japan Goes?" 1998. *The Economist*, June 20.

Audretsch, D. 1989. *The Market and the State*. New York: New York University Press.

"Backwards and Forwards in China." 1999. *The Economist* (editorial), March 13, pp. 71–72.

Ballon, R. 1997. "Stake-holders and Japanese Enterprise." *Journal of Japanese Trade & Industry*, No. 1.

Beckhart, H. B. (ed.). 1954. *Banking Systems*. New York: Columbia University Press.

Berger, M. 1994. "Renaissance: The Making of the Japanese Corporation." *Business Week*, July 11.

Bernstein, P. 1998. *Against the Gods: The Remarkable Story of Risk*. New York: John Wiley & Sons.

Blustein, P. 1992. "In Japan, All Eyes Are on the Bottom Line." *Washington Post*, March 23–29.

———. 1993. "Japan, Poised on the Brink of Eventual Change." *Washington Post*, July 26–August 1.

Brean, D.J.S. (ed.). 1998. *Taxation in Modern China*. New York: Routledge.

Bremner, B., and Thornton, E. 1998. "Bad Banks: Why Japan's Pols Are Paralyzed." *Business Week*, October 5.

Burstein, D. 1988. *Yen! Japan's Financial Empire and Its Threat to America*. New York: Simon & Schuster.

Chang, H. G., and Hou, J. 1997. "Structural Inflation and the 1994 'Monetary' Crisis in China." *Contemporary Economic Policy*, Vol. 15 (July), p. 81.

"China: Red Chips No More." 1998. *Business Week* (editorial), October 26.

China Finance Society. Various years. *Almanac of China's Finance and Banking*. Beijing: China Financial Publishing House.

Cohen, A. 1993. "Japan in Transit: Modeling the Japanese Corporation." *Management Japan*, Vol. 6, No. 2 (Autumn).

Cole, R. 1992. "Work and Leisure in Japan." *California Management Review* (Spring).

Davies, G. 1994. *A History of Money: From Ancient Times to the Present Day*. Cardiff: University of Wales Press.

De Silva, N. 1996. "Hashimoto Faces Mammoth Task to Drag His Nation Out of Economic and Social and Social Morass." *Hong Kong Standard*, January 11.

Denison, E., and Chung, W. K. 1976. *How Japan's Economy Grew So Fast: The Sources of Postwar Expansion*. Washington, DC: Brookings Institution.

Doherty, J. 1998a. "Trading Points: Japan Woes Affect US Loan Market: Starwood-ITT Deal." *Barron's*, Vol. 78, No. 3 (January).

———. 1998b. "Trading Points: Offer by Japan's Capital-Starved Sumitomo to Yield-Hungry US Investors Makes Everyone Happy." *Barron's*, Vol. 78, No. 6 (February).

Dore, R. 1994. "Japan in Recession." *Dollars and Sense*, Vol. 192 (March–April).

Economic Planning Agency, Government of Japan. 1995. *Economic Survey: 1993–94: A Challenge to New Frontiers Beyond the Severe Adjustment Process*. Tokyo: Economic Planning Agency, Government of Japan.

Fagerberg, J. 1994. "Technology and International Differences in Growth Rates." *Journal of Economic Literature*, Vol. 32 (September), pp. 1147–1175.

Fingleton, E. 1995. *Blindside: Why Japan Is Still on Track to Overtake the US by the Year 2000*. Boston: Houghton Mifflin.

Flamm, K. 1991. "Making New Rules." *The Brookings Review* (Spring).

Francks, P. 1992. *Japanese Economic Development: Theory and Practice*. London: Routledge.

"From Miracle to Mid-Life Crisis." 1993. *The Economist*, March 6.

Fry, M. 1998. "Can Seigniorage Income Keep China's Financial System Afloat?" In D.J.S. Brean (ed.), *Taxation in Modern China*. New York: Routledge.

Gilley, B. 1998. "Breaking the Bank." *Far Eastern Review*, July 16, pp. 66–68.

Harding, H. 1987. *China's Second Revolution: Reform After Mao*. Washington, DC: Brookings Institution.

Hartcher, P. 1998. *The Ministry: How Japan's Most Powerful Institution Endangers World Markets*. Boston: Harvard Business School Press.

Hay, D. et al. 1994. *Economic Reform and State-Owned Enterprises in China*. New York: Clarendon Press.

Honda, K. 1993. "New Style Corporate Governance Needed." *The Nikkei Weekly*, May 31.

Horvat, A. 1998. "MOF Fries in 'No Pan Shabu Shabu.' " *Euromoney* (March), pp. 40–42.

"How the Mob Burned the Banks." 1996. *Business Week* (editorial), January 29.

Hsiao, K. H. 1971. *Money and Monetary Policy in Communist China*. New York: Columbia University Press.

Huang, Y., and Duncan, R. 1997. "Which Chinese State-Owned Enterprises Make Loss?" *Journal of Economics and Business*, Vol. 1, No. 2 (December), pp. 41–51.

Hulten, C. 1990. *Productivity Growth in Japan and the United States*. Chicago: University of Chicago Press.

Ichimura, S., James, W., and Ramstetter, E. 1998. "The Financial Crisis in East Asia." *Journal of Economics and Business*, Vol. 2, No. 1 (June), pp. 1–43.

Ikeo, K. 1999. "Bank Regulation and Management Incentives: Implications for Japan." *Journal of Economics and Business*, Vol. 2, No. 1 (June), pp. 45–61.

International Monetary Fund (IMF). 1980. *World Economic Outlook*. Washington, DC: IMF.

Irvine, S. 1998. "Why Japanese Banks Don't Care for Profits." *Euromoney*, No. 346 (February).

Ito, T., and Iwaisako, T. 1996. "Explaining Asset Bubbles in Japan." *BOJ Monetary and Economic Studies*, Vol. 14, No. 1 (July), pp. 144–191.

Japan External Trade Organization (JETRO). 1994. *Tradescope*, Vol. 14, No. 4 (April).

"The Japan Puzzle." 1998. *The Economist* (editorial), March 21, pp. 15–27.

"Japanese Banks: Bad Analogies." 1998. *The Economist* (editorial), July 4–10.

"Japan's Economic Plight: Fallen Idol." 1998. *The Economist*, June 20.

Jordan, M. 1997. "$200 Billion Plan for Japan's Banks." *International Herald Tribune*, July 3.

Keizai Koho Center. 1991. *Japan in 1990: An International Comparison*. Tokyo: JETRO.

Kim, S., and Singer, R. 1997. "US and Japanese Banks: A Comparative Study." *The Bankers Magazine* (March–April), pp. 56–61.

Kime, K. 1998. "Seigniorage, Domestic Debt, and Financial Reform in China." *Contemporary Economic Policy*, Vol. 16, pp. 12–21.

Kindleberger, C. 1984. *A Financial History of Western Europe*. London: George Allen & Unwin.

——. 1989. *Manias, Panics, and Crashes: A History of Financial Crises* (2nd ed.). New York: Basic Books.

King, F. 1965. *Money and Monetary Policy in China: 1845–1895*. Cambridge, MA: Harvard University Press.

Kiyama, Y., Yamashita, T., Yoshida, T., and Yoshida, T. 1998. "Interest Rate Risk of Banking Accounts: Measuring Using the VAR Framework." *Monetary and Economic Studies* (May), pp. 1–32.

Kumar, A., Lardy, N., Abrecht, W., Chuppe, T., Selwyn, S., and Zhang, T. 1998. *China's Non-Bank Financial Institutions: Trust and Investment Companies.* World Bank Discussion Paper No. 358. Washington, DC: The World Bank.

Kunio, Y. 1979. *Japanese Economic Development.* Tokyo: Tokyo University Press.

Kuroki, Y. 1999. "Noisy Signals, Credit Rationing, and Bank Asset Quality." *Journal of Economics, Business, and Law,* Vol. 1, pp. 33–61.

Kynge, J. 1988. "China Unveils Further Cut in Interest Rates." *Financial Times,* July 1.

Lardy, N. 1996. "Foreign Trade and investment in China." *The Brookings Review,* Vol. 14, No. 1 (Winter).

Lawrence, S. 1998. "Unfinished Business." *Far Eastern Economic Review,* December 17, pp. 22–23.

Lazonick, W., and O'Sullivan, M. 1997. "Finance and Industrial Development: Evolution to Market Control. Part II: Japan and Germany." *Financial History Review,* Vol. 4, pp. 117–138.

Leggett, K. 1998. "Making a Market." *Wall Street Journal,* April 30.

Li, S., and Zhu, T. 1998. "China, Too, Faces Financial Perils." *Wall Street Journal,* October 28.

Ling, Z., Zhongyi, J., and von Braun, J. 1997. *Credit Systems for the Rural Poor in China.* Commack, NY: Nova Science Publishers.

"Loan Crisis Makes Clear the Need to Overhaul Finance Ministry." 1996. *Nikkei Weekly* (editorial), February 19, p. 65.

Lu, D., and Yu, Q. 1998. "Banking Credit-Quota Plan as a Macroeconomic Policy Instrument in China: Effectiveness and Costs." *Economic Systems,* Vol. 22, No. 2 (June), pp. 147–174.

McAlinn, G. P. 1998. "Financial Reform in Japan: The Big Bang." *Asia Business Law Review,* No. 22 (October), pp. 3–11.

———. 1999. "Financial Crisis in Japan: The Big Bang." *Asia Business Law Review,* No. 23 (January), pp. 3–11.

Melloan, G. 1996. "How Japan's Goblin's Spook Wall Street." *Wall Street Journal,* March 10.

Mitchell, A. 1997. "Can the 'Big Bang' Change Japan?" *The Bankers Magazine* (March–April), pp. 5–11.

Mookerjee, R., and Peebles, G. 1998. "Endogenous Money in China: Evidence and Insights on Recent Policies." *Journal of Asian Economics,* Vol. 9, No. 1, pp. 139–158.

Morita, A. 1992. "A Critical Moment for Japanese Management." *Economic Eye,* Vol. 13, No. 3 (August), pp. 12–17.

Mourdoukoutas, P. 1993. *Japan's Turn: The Interchange in Economic Leadership.* Lanham, MD: University Press of America.

———. 1995. *Strategy ADP: How to Compete in the Japanese Market.* Boston: Copley Publishing Group.

————. 1999a. *Collective Entrepreneurship in a Globalizing Economy*. Westport, CT: Quorum Books.

————. 1999b. *The Global Corporation: The Decolonization of International Business*. Westport, CT: Quorum Books.

Naoki, T. 1998. "The Importance of Financial Self-Governance." *Japan Echo*, Vol. 25, No. 3 (April), pp. 44–49.

Neumann, M. 1996. "A Comparative Study of Seigniorage: Japan and Germany." *BOJ Monetary and Economic Studies*, Vol. 14, No. 1 (July), pp. 105–135.

Noble, G. 1993. "Japan in 1992: Just Another Aging Superpower?" *Asian Survey* (January).

Nukazawa, K. 1998. "The Japanese Economy: From World War II to the New Economy." *Japan Echo*, Vol. 25, No. 3 (April), pp. 36–42.

Office of Economic Cooperation and Development (OECD). 1984. *Economic Surveys: Japan*. Paris: OECD.

————. 1985. *Economic Surveys: Japan*. Paris: OECD.

————. 1989. *Economies in Transition*. Paris: OECD.

————. 1992. *Economic Observer*, No. 174 (June–July).

————. 1993. *Economic Surveys: Japan*. Paris: OECD.

————. 1994a. *Economic Outlook*. Paris: OECD.

————. 1994b. *Economic Surveys: Japan*. Paris: OECD.

————. 1995. *Economic Surveys: Japan*. Paris: OECD.

————. 1996. *Economic Surveys: Japan*. Paris: OECD.

————. 1997. *Economic Surveys: Japan*. Paris: OECD.

Olson, M. 1982. *The Rise and Decline of Nations*. New Haven, CT: Yale University Press.

"On a Wing and a Prayer." 1999. *The Economist*, April 17, pp. 3–25.

Pressnell, L. S. (ed.). 1973. *Money and Banking in Japan*. New York: St. Martin's Press.

Reed, S. 1996. "Japan: The Banking Scandal Could Hamstring Hashimoto." *Business Week*, February 5, p. 65.

Reinebach, A. 1998. "Japan's Capital-Hungry Banks Look to the Growing CLO Market." *Investment Dealers Digest*, Vol. 64, No. 1 (February 16), p. 26.

Rohwer, J. 1998. "Yikes! Japan's Bank Debt Is Scarier Than You Think." *Fortune*, November 9, p. 18.

Rosenbluth, M. F. 1989. *Financial Politics in Contemporary Japan*. Ithaca, NY: Cornell University Press.

Sakuya, F. 1998. "Japan's Financial Woes and the Hopes for Big Bang." *Japan Echo*, Vol. 25, No. 1 (February), pp. 18–25.

Sapsford, J. 1995a. "Japan Unveils Plan to End Banking Crisis That Could Clear the Way from Failure." *Wall Street Journal*, June 9, p. A2.

————. 1995b. "Tokyo Concedes Broader Banking Crisis." *Wall Street Journal*, August 1.

————. 1995c. "Tokyo Hits a Wall with Economic Plans." *Wall Street Journal*, June 28, p. A3.

————. 1996a. "Japan's Tokai Bank Sets Big Write-Off in Bid to Put Industry Crisis Behind." *Wall Street Journal*, February 29, p. A3.

————. 1996b. "Many Japanese Companies to Report Losses." *Wall Street Journal*, February 21.

————. 1998. "Good Loans at Bad Banks Vex Japanese." *Wall Street Journal*, August 20, p. A4.

Sato, S. 1998. "Asian Financial Crisis." *Japan and the World Economy*, Vol. 10, pp. 371–375.

Saywell, T., and Jiangsu, K. 1999. "On the Edge." *Far Eastern Economic Review*, February 25, pp. 46–49.

Sender, H. 1992. "Facing the World: Japan's Humbled Brokers Adopt a Global Outlook." *Far Eastern Economic Review*, November 26, p. 25.

"Shellshocked by the Yen, Japanese Companies Still Find Ways to Cope." 1995. *New York Times* (cover story), April 18.

Shikano, Y. 1998. "Distinctive Features of the Japanese Main Bank Relationship in a Comparative Perspective." *Japanese Journal of Financial Economics*, Vol. 2, No. 1 (January), pp. 79–100.

Shishido, S., and Nakajima, T. 1999. "Asian Currency Crisis and the Role of Japan." *The Developing Economies*, Vol. 36, No. 1 (March), pp. 3–34.

Silk, Leonard, and Kono, T. 1993. "Sayonara, Japan Inc." *Foreign Policy*, Vol. 93 (Winter), p. 18.

Smith, C. 1994. "Economic Monitor: Japan Still in Recession." *Far Eastern Economic Review*, January 27, p. 42.

Smith, C., and Leggett, K. 1999. "Chinese Face More Defaults by State Firms." *Wall Street Journal*, February 1.

State Statistical Bureau. Various years. *China Statistical Yearbook*. Beijing: China Statistical Publishing House.

Statistics Bureau, Japan Statistical Association. Various years. *Statistical Yearbook of Japan*. Tokyo: Japan Statistical Association.

Stevenson, R. 1998. "Tailoring the S & L Crisis to Save Japan's Banks." *New York Times*, October 18.

Storm, S. 1998. "Messages by Clinton and Rubin Reverberate in Asia." *International Herald Tribune*, July 2.

Suzuki, Y. 1980. *Money and Banking in Contemporary Japan*. New Haven, CT: Yale University Press.

————. 1996. "The Main Issues Facing Japan's Economy." *Japan and the World Economy*, Vol. 8.

Suzuki, Y. (ed.). 1987. *The Japanese Financial System*. Oxford: Clarendon Press.

Tanaka, N. 1998. "The Importance of Self-Governance." *Japan Echo*, Vol. 25, No. 3 (April).

Telt, G. 1998a. "EBRD May Cut Credit to Japan's Banks." *Financial Times*, August 20.

————. 1998b. "Japan in 4,000 bln Sales of Bad Loans." *Financial Times*, August 19.

Thornton, E. 1994a. "Deregulation Dawdle." *Far Eastern Economic Review*, September 29.

———. 1994b. "Revolution in Japanese Retailing." *Fortune*, February 7.

Tsuru, S. 1993. *Japan's Capitalism: Creative Defeat and Beyond*. Cambridge, MA: Cambridge University Press.

Watanabe, T. 1998. "Lessons of the Southeast Asian Meltdown." *Japan Echo*, Vol. 25, No. 3 (April).

Wei, S., and Zeckhauser, R. 1998. "Two Crises and Two Chinas." *Japan and the World Economy*, Vol. 10, pp. 359–369.

White, L. 1991. *The S&L Debacle: Public Policy Lessons for Bank and Thrift Regulation*. New York: Oxford University Press.

Whitman, M. 1998. "Japan Should Write a New Chapter." *Barron's*, October 19.

Williams, M. 1996. "Revolving Door: Many Japanese Companies Ran Amok While Led by Former Regulators." *Wall Street Journal*, January 19.

Wood, C. 1992. *The Bubble Economy*. New York: Atlantic Monthly Press.

WuDunn, S. 1999. "Why Japan Is Rooting for China." *New York Times*, March 7, Week in Review Section, p. 4.

Xu-Yao, Q., Ke-Chun, Y., and Chan-Min, X. 1989. "An Evolutionary Account of Management Development in China." In Julia Davies, Mark Easterby-Smith, Sara Mann, and Morgan Tandon (eds.), *The Challenge to Western Management: International Alternatives*. London: Routledge.

Yamazawa, K. 1998. "The Asian Economic Crisis and Japan." *The Developing Economies*, Vol. 36, No. 3 (September), pp. 332–351.

Yamori, N. 1998. "Bureaucrat-Managers and Corporate Governance: Expense-Preference Behaviors in Japanese Financial Institutions." *Economic Letters*, Vol. 61, pp. 385–389.

Yanagihara, T. 1994. "Japan as a Newly-Industrializing Country." *Journal of International and Economic Studies*, No. 8.

Yang, Y., and Zhong, C. 1998. "China's Textile and Clothing Exports in a Changing Economy." *The Developing Economies*, Vol. 36, No. 1 (March), pp. 3–23.

Yen, Chi-Wa. 1998. "The Fifth Dragon: Sources of Growth in Guangdong, 1979–1994." *Contemporary Economic Policy*, Vol. 14 (January), pp. 1–11.

Yu, Q., and Xie, P. 1999. "Money Aggregates Management: Problems and Prospects in China's Economic Transition." *Contemporary Economic Policy*, Vol. 17 (January), pp. 33–43.

Zhang, P. 1998. "China's Coming Economic Crisis." *The New Australian*, No. 95 (November 9–15), pp. 1–2.

Index

Abacus banking, 1, 6–7, 14, 59, 164, 167
  conditions, 6–7, 8, 10, 12, 14, 164
Amakundori, 45–46
Annual growth rates of loans to
    SOEs, 159, 160
Asian crisis, 128–132
Assets managed per bank worker, 9

Bank of Japan (BOJ), 2, 20, 32, 34, 69,
    79, 93, 97
Bank profitability, 32, 37, 38, 78, 90
Banker's guilds, 105, 106
Banks' long-term relations, 10, 34, 35,
    36
Bogai, 79, 80
Boxer Rebellion, 104

Central planning, 141, 142, 163
China
  bank assets, 117, 118
  bank deposits, 121
  bank loans, 114, 115
  bank management, 123, 124, 125,
    151

bank net loans, 153, 154, 157, 159
bubble economy, 157, 159
budget deficit, 148, 149
development, 102, 103, 104
domestic market, 132, 133
excess capacity, 156, 158
export unit values, 134, 135
fall of abacus banking, 148, 149, 159
financial assets, 119, 120, 154, 156
financial deregulation, 113, 114, 157,
    159
financial organization, 108, 112, 159
foreign direct investment, 108, 109,
    136
foreign trade, 108, 110, 136, 137
government revenues, 150, 151, 152
high-growth period, 102, 103
inability to innovate, 133, 134
looming banking crisis, 6, 13, 145,
    146, 149, 151, 159, 164, 168–169
market frontier, 128, 129, 132
money supply, 141, 142
production and employment, 154,
    157

real GDP growth, 108, 111, 137, 138
reforms, 102, 108, 109, 151, 152, 153,
    156, 159, 163
rise of abacus banking, 101, 102, 105
savings, 114, 115, 152
state banking system, 123, 124, 153,
    156, 159
Core banks, 84–85
Credit collectives, 153–154
Credit funds balance sheet, 140, 141
Credit rating, 73, 74, 75, 77
Credit risk, 32–33
Cultural Revolution, 104, 105

Debt-to-equity ratios, 149, 150
Deflation, 133, 134

Excess capacity, 158–159
Excessive duplication, 158–159

Fall of abacus banking
    in China, 148, 149, 159
    in Japan, 17, 53, 71, 164
Fuji Bank, 5–6

Gene-con, 82, 83
Glass-Steagall Act, 20, 32, 41
Gosou-sendan Houshiki, 42, 43, 44, 48
    disbanding of, 69, 70, 87, 88
Guangdong International Trust Cor-
    poration (GITC), 5, 146, 147

Hianan Development Bank, 158, 159
Hollowing out, 62, 63
Hyperliquidity, 11, 54, 59, 78, 80, 90,
    163, 165

Institutional changes, 14
Interest rate controls, 159–160
Interest rate spread, 8, 60, 61, 159
International Trust and Investment
    Corporations (ITICs), 13, 119, 120,
    140, 141, 146, 153, 156, 159
    Fujan ITIC, 140, 147–148

Shandong ITIC, 146–148
Shanghai ITIC, 148
Shenzen ITIC, 148
Tianjin ITIC, 148

Japan
    bank governance, 4, 20, 21, 34, 163
    bank loans, 30
    banking crisis, 2, 6, 13, 17, 73, 75,
        79, 90, 91
    banking deregulation, 4, 54, 55, 56,
        57, 58, 66, 67, 163, 166–167
    banking regulation, 4, 40, 41, 42, 45,
        163
    export-led industrialization, 2, 22,
        23, 34, 47, 54, 55, 73
    "extended high-growth" era, 14, 21,
        33
    fall of abacus banking, 17, 53, 71, 164
    financial intermediation ratio, 25, 26
    industrial policy, 47, 73, 163
    industrialization, 7, 21, 22, 23, 34
    investment in Asia, 62–63
    rise of abacus banking, 17, 18, 25
    savings, 25–26
Japan Resolution Trust Corporation
    (JRTC), 4, 5
Jusen, 11–12, 77, 78, 80, 81, 82, 88–90,
    160

Keiretsu, 20, 37, 39, 69, 79, 165, 167

Loan syndicates, 84–85
Loans outstanding, 80, 81, 159

Main bank, 22, 36, 39, 84, 85
Market risks, 20, 32, 34, 48
Ministry of Finance (MOF), 1–4, 6, 7,
    37, 41, 42, 45, 69, 71, 79, 87, 88,
    93, 97–99
Ministry of International Trade and
    Industry (MITI), 1–2, 6–8, 20, 39,
    40
Mitsui Real Estate, 11–12

Moody's credit rating for selective
    ITICs, 145, 146

Non-bank financial enterprises, 102,
    103, 159
Non-performing assets, 1, 3, 11, 151,
    153

Occupation, 21, 22
Overloading, 20, 24, 29, 32, 34

Passive-volume lending, 164–165
People's Bank of China, 105, 106, 107,
    108, 117, 119, 123, 158
Plaza Accord, 65, 66, 78, 79, 80, 166–
    167
Policy of Enriched Industrialization, 7
Price destruction, 133, 134

Quing dynasty, 101–102

Rise of abacus banking
    in China, 101, 102, 105
    in Japan, 17, 18, 25
Risk management, 79, 80

Sakura Bank, 5–6
Securities and Exchange Law of 1948,
    41–42

Seigniorage, 113, 151–153
Selective bank downgrades, 146, 147
Song dynasty, 104, 105
Speculative mania, 73, 74, 75, 149–150,
    162
State-owned enterprises (SOEs), 12,
    13, 101, 102, 108, 109, 117, 119,
    123, 124, 126, 131, 147, 148, 149,
    151, 159, 165–166
    bank financing, 137, 138, 146, 147,
    148, 153, 159
    profits, 138, 139, 153
Sumitomo Bank, 5–6, 77

Taiping Rebellion, 105–106
Township and village enterprises
    (TVEs), 150, 151

United States
    demands on China, 130, 131, 151
    trade deficit with China, 129, 130

World Trade Organization (WTO), 13,
    65, 129, 130

Yamaichi Corporation, 37–38
Yishida Doctrine, 23, 24, 56

Zaibatsu, 21–22
Zeitek, 11, 81, 82, 85

About the Authors

YUKO ARAYAMA began his career at Nagoya University, where he teaches and conducts research in economic theory and applied economics. Professor Arayama has visited Beijing University several times since 1991, and he currently serves as the Director of the Contemporary Japanese Economic Research Program. He is the author of several articles presented in academic and business conferences and published in professional journals, and is co-author, with Panos Mourdoukoutas, of *China Against Herself: Innovation or Imitation in Global Business?* (Quorum Books, 1999).

PANOS MOURDOUKOUTAS began his career at the State University of Pennsylvania and currently teaches at Long Island University in New York. He has traveled extensively throughout Asia and Europe, and has spent a great deal of time at Nagoya University in Japan. He has been an advisor to government and business organizations and has published several articles and books, including *Beating the Market: How to Win the Wall Street Game, Collective Entrepreneurship in a Globalizing Economy, The Global Corporation: The Decolonization of International Businesses, Japan's Turn: The Interchange in Economic Leadership, Strategy ADP: How to Compete in the Japanese Market*, and *The Experiment*. He has also co-authored *China Against Herself* and *Japanese Management and Marketing* (in Greek).